AYLSHAM INNS AND PUBLIC HOUSES
— *A HISTORY*

Elizabeth Gale

First published in Great Britain 2001 by Elizabeth Gale and Aylsham Local History Society.

© Elizabeth Gale

All rights reserved. No part of this book may be reproduced or transmitted in any form or by any means, electronic or mechanical, including photocopying, recording, or by any information storage and retrieval system, without permission from the author.

ISBN 0-9521564-8-2

Printed in Great Britain by Catton Print, Norwich.

AYLSHAM INNS AND PUBLIC HOUSES
— *A HISTORY*

Contents

	Page
List of illustrations	iv
Preface and Acknowledgements	v
List of Contributors	vi
Aylsham	1-7
The Establishment of Inns and Public Houses	9-12
The Black Boys	13-22
The Unicorn	23-28
The Half Moon Inn	29-30
The Swan	31-32
The Feathers	33-35
The Dog	36-42
Aylsham Manor	43-44
The Angel Inn	45-47
The Bull Inn	48-49
The New Inn and King's Head	50-54
The Cross Keys	55-57
The Star Inn	58-59
The Red Lion	60-65
The Ship	66-68
The White Hart Inn	69-72
The Brewery	73-75
The White Horse	76-78
The Stonemasons	79-84
The Anchor Inn	85-91
The Royal Oak	92-95
Aylsham's Vanished Inns and Public Houses	96-97
Inn and Public House Signs	98-101
Brewers and Breweries	102-108
References	109-110
Index	111-118

List of Illustrations

	Page
A Caution to Innkeepers and others	8
Map of Inns and Public Houses in Aylsham	12
Black Boys advertisements for 1880 and 1909	18
Black Boys advertisement 1923	19
Window from the Black Boys	21
The Black Boys in 1928 and 2001	22
The Unicorn Bowling Team 1907	25
Advertisement for the Unicorn 1 968	27
The Unicorn in 1964 and 2001	28
The former Half Moon Inn	30
The Swan in 1965	32
The Feathers in 1938 and 2001	35
Advertisements for the Dog in 1909 and 1936	39
The Dog Inn Estate in 1855	40
The Dog bowling green team in 1900 and team in 1910	42
Poem by W.M. Mileham celebrating Oakapple Day	53
Plan of New Inn prior to 1953	54
The Cross Keys	57
Site of Star Inn in 1995	59
Red Lion 1972	63
Former Red Lion 1995	65
The Ship 1902 and 1970	68
Former White Hart 1970	72
Former Brewery	74
Bill from Samuel Ducker 1891	75
The Former White Horse	78
Bill from John Freeman 1854	80
Annie Frances Laxen/Bullock	82
The Stonemasons Quoits learn in 1911	83
The Stonemasons in 1970 and 1995	84
Plan of the Anchor Inn 1962	86
Anchor Inn in the 1900's and in 1962	88
Painting of the Anchor Inn in 1850 & Bridge House in 1995	90
The Royal Oak	94
Maidens Bower	95
Aylsham Inn signs	98

PREFACE & ACKNOWLEDGEMENTS

This book is the outcome of research into the past and present history of the inns and public houses in Aylsham, Norfolk. Inevitably there are gaps, due to a lack of written documentation or because relevant records have been destroyed. In some instances the names of publicans have been found, but not those of the owners.

These establishments changed their titles over the years from beerhouse, public house, inn or hotel. Those who administered these premises were known variously as innkeeper, victualler, landlord, landlady, proprietor or publican. The latter title is appropriate to both male and female and I have chosen to use this term throughout the book. All the inns and public houses are written of according to their location in Aylsham so that the reader can easily identify the sites, many of which were closed together.

I am grateful to Ron Peabody, former Hon. Aylsham Archivest and Tom Mollard, editor of the Aylsham Local History Society for their help with my research. The Aylsham Town Council have generously given their permission for documents and photographs from the Aylsham Archives to be reproduced. The Aylsham Association have kindly given permission for the reproduction of some photographs.

Many residents have answered my questions, supplied information, photographs and plans. In addition I have been in contact with non-residents who have been researching their family history and they have given many of the details. Some members of the Aylsham Local History Society have passed on useful information which they have found in their own personal history research. I appreciate receiving all this assistance from everyone.

I am indebted to Nesta Evans from the University of East Anglia for her guidance, advice and helpful suggestions regarding the text. Last, but not least, my thanks are due to my husband for the drawings, many photographs and for his encouragement throughout the writing of this book.

Elizabeth Gale

LIST OF CONTRIBUTORS

Derrick Baker
June Bedder
Margaret Bird
T.W. Bishop
Maureen Burr
N. Crick
Geoffrey Ducker
Joan Ducker
Jack and Mary Edmonds
Peter and Paula Farrand
Pauline Hagon
W.N. Hopcroft
Jill Kemp
Marilyn Laxen
Melvin Laxen
Molly Long
Derek Lyons
Diana Newstead
Enid Parry
Alan Rowlands
Barry and Pat Waller
Tom West

AYLSHAM

The market town of Aylsham in Norfolk is situated near the River Bure, twelve miles north of Norwich and eleven miles from Cromer. There is evidence of a small settlement of the Late Iron Age (c300 BC-43 AD) near to Aylsham and flint axes and arrowheads have been found in other areas dating to the New Stone Age (c2500-1700 BC). East Anglia was subjected to occupation by the Romans until they left in 400 AD and were followed by the Saxons.

Somewhere around 500 AD, a Saxon named Aegel, set up a homestead with his family and followers near to the present market place. This settlement was called Aegel's Ham, the term Ham meaning a homestead and this was the first name of the present town. Aegel's descendants probably occupied the site for three hundred years until they were displaced by the Danes. The name of this Saxon settlement was however retained and in the Domesday Book of 1086, it is recorded as Elesham, but in the 1500s the spelling was given as Ailesham or Aylesham and subsequently became Aylsham. The population increased as the town became established and although early figures have not been authentically recorded, by 1751 there were 1,230 inhabitants. In 1881, this number had risen to 2,674 and the present day figure is 5,420.

The centre of Aylsham is the Market Place, a large open square with shops on all four sides and with accommodation above. In medieval times, traders set up stalls to sell their wares on market days and this practice has continued to the present day although most of the square has now been designated as car parking areas. For many years, the market place was the venue for celebrating Royal events, the end of wars, national holidays, fairs and circuses. The Town Hall, built in 1857 and extended in 1892, stands at the north east corner and is used for Town Council meetings, various social events and also contains the Aylsham Archives where many documents and books relating to the history of the town are stored.

At the northern end of the market place is the church of St Michael, built of flint and stone and a fine example of craftsmanship. It dates from 1380 when John of Gaunt, Duke of Lancaster, contributed financially to the building and wealthy patrons gave financial support while others provided materials or labour. Many changes, particularly in the Victorian era, have been made to the interior of the church since it was first constructed. The floor has inlaid slabs denoting the burial places of many Aylsham's past prominent residents. On the walls are tablets and monumental plaques erected in memory of other former inhabitants and to the young men who lost their lives in many wars. The church has a spire, a clock and ten bells in the belfry, which are rung for Sunday services and wedding ceremonies. A graveyards surrounds the church and contains stone memorials to many of the town's former residents. Humphrey Repton, the landscape designer who died in 1818 is interred near to one wall of the church and his grave is marked with a stone memorial.

Apart from St Michael's, other churches were established in the town. One was the Baptist Church in 1790, but it did not have a regular preacher and relied on preachers coming to Aylsham from Norwich. A suitable building was found off White Hart Street which was enlarged in 1825. The first pastor was the Rev. Joseph Bane who held the position for 31 years. This Baptist Church is now known as the Emmanuel Church.

Methodism came to Aylsham early in the nineteenth century and religious meetings were either held in the open air, in suitable buildings or in private houses. By 1841, the Wesleyan Methodists had a chapel in White Hart Street and the present one dates from 1883 with renovations carried out in the early 1900s. The Primitive Methodists worshipped in a chapel in Mill Road, but this was closed in 1932 and the congregation moved to the White Hart Street chapel. Another denomination was the Wesleyan Reform Union who built a church in Millgate which was called the Tabernacle. This building has since closed as a place of worship and a new church was built in the Norwich Road.

Roman Catholics have a church on the corner of White Hart Street and Gas House Hill. The original building was very small and was built by the Shepheard family, who were devout Roman Catholics. In later years an extension was added to enlarge the original building. Another long established church is the Salvation Army which was founded in 1885. They acquired the former schoolroom of Dr. Ager's Collegiate School and continue to the present day in these premises. For many years, the Quakers who lived in Aylsham, had to travel to Norwich for their meetings. In 1994, they purchased a building in Pegg's Yard off Red Lion Street as a meeting house.

On the corner of Red Lion Street and Burgh Road is the former Bridewell. It was erected by Robert Marsham in 1543 as a house of correction for vagabonds and prostitutes, but later became a lock up and prison. In 1787, the building was re-built and its use as a prison ended in 1825 when prisoners were transferred to Norwich and it is now a private house.

One of the main attractions for Aylsham residents and visitors is the water mill situated on the River Bure at Millgate. A mill on this site is recorded in the Domesday Book and there were probably several re-buildings over the centuries. By the early 1700s, the mill had fallen into disrepair and was re-built by Robert Parmeter in the mid 1700s. Aylsham had two brick tower windmills which were probably built in 1826 and one was situated at the rear of 5 Mill Road. The sails were blown off in a gale on the 24th March 1895 and the mill was not used again. It was demolished in 1941. The other windmill was in the Cawston Road and was struck by lightening in 1900, causing damage to the sails. This incident put the mill out of use and twenty years later, a heavy gale removed the cap and sails. The rest of the tower survived, it is now privately owned and has been converted into holiday accommodation.

In the early part of the 18th century, a scheme was proposed to make a canal from Coltishall to the Staithe at Aylsham which would allow wherries to transport cargoes along this waterway to the mill. It was an expensive enterprise and after many difficulties, not only financially, but with contractors, the canal was eventually finished in late 1779. Wherries sailed along this navigation canal and brought goods to Aylsham and increased the prosperity of the town until the great flood of 1912 destroyed the locks and silted up the canal bed. The cost of repairing the damage was too much for the Commissioners of the Navigation Company and, as government aid was not forthcoming, it heralded the demise of the wherry trading vessels to the Aylsham water mill.

The railways came to Aylsham in the mid 1800s and two stations were built, one at the southern end of the town and the other at the north end at Millgate. These railway lines were closed by Dr. Richard Beeching, Chairman of British Railways, in the 1950s and the south station was converted to run miniature trains between Aylsham and Wroxham, and is now known as the Bure Valley Railway. The railway lines at the northern end of the town were removed, the station and signal box were demolished and the old railway track is now a part of the Weavers Way. Before the railways, the means of travel were on horseback, by horse and cart or by public coach services with pick up and setting down points at Aylsham's principal inns. The wealthier had traps or carriages and a few had their own private coach. With the invention of the motor car and motorised omnibuses, the mode of travelling changed and many of the trades associated with horses disappeared from Aylsham.

The development of Aylsham principally dates to the medieval period when many cottages, tenements and houses were built. These early buildings have vanished, but many dating to the 1500s and 1600s have survived, some of which are built on the foundations of earlier sites. Tenements were built close together and were the homes of the poorest in the town, who lived in overcrowded conditions. For those who were destitute, their home was the workhouse and the first in the town was situated in the angle between what is now Bure Way and New Road in Millgate. It was built in 1776 and demolished in 1842 when a larger workhouse was erected on a site of about twelve acres on the Cawston Road in 1849. This workhouse closed in 1948, the residents were moved to County Council homes and the building was converted into St Michael's Hospital.

Many large houses were built on the periphery of the town by those who were wealthy and have since become buildings of historic note and it is worth mentioning a few. Norfolk House in Hungate Street dates to the 1700s and may be older and has in recent years been renovated. On the Blickling Road are two large houses of architectural merit. One is The Knoll containing early 18th century panelling and the James Wright map of 1839 lists an Old Bowling Green in the grounds. The other is West Lodge, said to have been built by the Marquess Townsend in about 1760. Further along the Blickling Road is the magnificent Blickling Hall dating to the 1600s, owned by the National Trust and visited by many during the tourist season.

Holman House is on the north side of the market place with its north facade facing directly into St Michael's churchyard. The house is a typical Regency building, built of red brick, two storeys in height and with sash windows. Research on the building has discovered an undercroft that dates to the medieval period and suggests that a building of some importance once stood on this site. For many years, this house was used as a medical practice by a group of doctors until they moved to a new purpose built building in the Norwich Road. The property was sold and the present owner has restored the house and preserved all the original features. Another building of merit is Dyes House situated on the west side of the market place. This property was formerly divided as offices for an estate agent and solicitor. These premises were sold and converted by the purchaser into a private residence. It is a timber framed building and thought to date to the 1500s and has a medieval cellar. During renovations, original beams with carpenters marks were exposed and now form a feature in the house.

On the north side of St Michael's churchyard, on the Cromer Road, is the Old Vicarage built in 1700 by the Rev. Jonathan Wrench which ceased to be a vicarage in 1956 and was sold the following year with part of the glebe land. Further along Cromer Road is The Grange, owned for many years by the Sapwell family and the residence of Dr. John Sapwell, the author of '*A History of Aylsham*'. Bushey House is another notable residence in the Cromer Road and dates to about 1855. It was occupied for many years by Dr. Richard Kay Morton and in subsequent years the building has been converted into an independent school.

White Hart Street has notable houses, Bayfield House and Abbot's House, the latter has been restored in recent years. Opposite Abbot's House is Cedar House, built in 1891 by William Starling. Situated at the corner of Gas House Hill and Sir William's Lane is The Belt Lodge, a small thatched building with an extension. This was the original lodge of the Belt Estate which had extensive lands and a house called The Belt, dating to the 1600s. The Belt is at the end of a private lane in Mill Row. At the corner of Mill Row and Millgate is Bure House which has the initials TR and the date 1768 carved into a brick on the south side of the house.

Confusingly in Drabblegate there are two houses called Abbot's Hall, almost opposite each other. The one on the west side is an old farmhouse, built in 1610 by Robert Wood and stands on or near the site of a manor house built by Abbot Sampson of Bury St Edmunds in 1190. The other Abbot's Hall on the east was erected by John Peterson in the 18th century. Philip Candler Shepheard purchased this residence along with farmland after his marriage to Maria Pasqua in 1881. The property later passed to his son Samuel and after his death, it was sold.

The inhabitants of Aylsham in its formative years were farmers, agricultural labourers and craftsmen and very few could read or write. Robert Jannys, a prosperous Norwich merchant and City Sheriff in 1509, was the first to set up a free school in Aylsham in 1517. Children received a basic education in reading, writing and arithmetic, but during harvest time many of these children were taken out of school to help gather in the crops. The increase in population since 1517 made it necessary to provide more schools for Aylsham children. Today there are pre-school nurseries and children in the town attend school from the age of five years until aged sixteen years. Their education can be continued in sixth form colleges, leading to higher education colleges and universities.

Those who were wealthier residents or prosperous farmers from the surrounding areas of Aylsham, were able to afford private education for their children and several fee paying schools were established in the town. One of these was at 27 Commercial Road (now Bure Way) and accommodated seventy boys of whom twenty were boarders. The headmaster was William Wright who founded the school in 1831 and it closed after his death in 1874; and is now a private residence. Another boys school was the Collegiate School at 64 Hungate Street with Dr. George Ager as the headmaster. There were six masters and 150 pupils aged from 14-19 years. This school eventually closed and is now the Royal British Legion ex-servicemens club. Girls with prosperous parents could also obtain a private education in the 1800s at the Gothic House in Hungate Street, which was administered by a Miss Roy. Another girls school was established by the Misses Chamberlain at The Beeches in Cawston Road. Both these former school buildings are now private residences.

From its early beginnings, the town grew and prospered and in the 14th century became famous for the weaving of a linen cloth known as Aylsham Web, Cloth of Aylsham, or Aylsham Linen or Canvas. The high quality of this cloth was appreciated not only in Norfolk, but throughout the kingdom and it was exported to France. By the 16th century, the demand for this cloth had declined and eventually it ceased to be produced.

Records show that in the 19th century many male inhabitants earned their living as agricultural labourers, saddle and harnessmakers, wheelwrights, blacksmiths, basket makers, coach and boat builders. Women were employed as domestic servants, straw bonnet makers, dressmakers, laundresses and shop assistants. The majority of these trades came to an end over the following years, but employment in agricultural work on farms on the fringes of Aylsham continued until mechanised farming brought an end to the need for so many workers.

From earliest times, the inhabitants of Aylsham obtained their water from streams or wells; the latter were sunk to a great depth, sometimes supplying one household or shared by a number of households. In 1938, the Norwich City Waterworks laid pipes along the Norwich and Aylsham roads and piped water came to the town. The installation of water to individual cottages and houses resulted in many homes having indoor toilets and bathrooms for the first time. The wells were filled in, the sites of many were not documented and a great deal of this information appears to have been lost. The lighting of homes and public buildings in early times had been by candlelight, superseded by oil lamps, but this changed when the Gas Light and Coke Company was formed in Aylsham in 1849 and a gasworks erected at the beginning of Millgate, now known as Gashouse Hill. The town centre was lit by gas, but this was not extended to the outlying areas until later. Gas lighting was replaced by electricity in 1929.

Since the 1950s, Aylsham has changed a great deal with the building of housing estates on what was formerly agricultural land. Millgate to the north was almost a village area, separated from the town by market gardens and fields. These areas have been built upon with houses and bungalows and Millgate is no longer a separate entity. To the north a large industrial estate has been established in and behind Dunkirk on what was formerly farmland. In recent years more housing has been built on the southern outskirts of the town and on small plots of land in between.

Despite the extensive expansion of Aylsham with new housing and supermarkets, the centre of the town still retains its market character and residents and visitors alike can enjoy all that this historic part of Norfolk has to offer. Many parts have been designated conservation areas and these are now preserved for present and future generations. Interwoven in the town's history are the inns and public houses that were, for many years, a part of the social life for the inhabitants.

A Caution

TO

INNKEEPERS

And Others.

WHEREAS every Innkeeper or Alehouse-keeper is by Act of Parliament subject to a Penalty, for suffering any person to continue Tippling in his house, and is also thereby disabled for the space of three years to keep an Alehouse.

And Whereas every person so Tippling, is also by the same Act, subject to a Penalty.

And Whereas, by another Act of Parliament, all persons who by neglecting to work, or by spending their money in Alehouses, cause their families to be Chargeable to their Parishes, are to be committed to the House of Correction, and there kept at hard labour.

Notice is hereby given,

That the AYLSHAM ASSOCIATION for PROTECTING PROPERTY and PREVENTING CRIMES, being convinced that Idleness and Drunkenness lead to crimes of every kind, will enforce the execution of the said Acts of Parliament, and will pursue such other measures as may be necessary, for bringing to justice all those who shall be guilty of such offences, as have lately been frequent in the Town and Neighbourhood.

And as it appears by the confession of almost all who are executed for Murders and other crimes, that Drunkenness, Bad Company, and Sabbath-breaking, were the first steps towards the Gallows. All Parents who have any regard for their children, either in this world or the next, are most solemnly advised to bring them up in habits of Honesty and Industry, and to keep them as much as possible from the Company of those whose advice or example would lead them into mischief.

Stevenson, Matchett, and Stevenson, Printers, Norwich.

A Caution to Innkeepers and Others.
(Copyright Aylsham Town Council)

THE ESTABLISHMENT OF INNS & PUBLIC HOUSES

The first to distribute ale and food to travellers were the monks and priests in monasteries and priories. Ale was brewed in these religious establishments from malt, mainly barley with water and yeast. King David of Kent in 695 AD was concerned about the monks and priests indulging too well in the drinking of ale and being incapable of carrying out their religious duties. He decreed:- 'If any priest is too drunk to discharge his duty, he shall abstain from his ministrations pending a decision from the Bishop'. Guests who stayed in these religious houses were not expected to pay for the hospitality that they received, but financial contributions from wealthier guests were always accepted.

In the years prior to the Norman invasion, a number of alehouses were in existence in towns and villages alongside former Roman roads. These were primitive huts with an earth floor and sparsely furnished with wooden benches and a few chairs. They were identifiable to the traveller by a long wooden pole, covered in evergreen branches which protruded near to the alehouse roof. The alehouses were mainly administered by women, who brewed the ale at the rear of the premises in buckets and for many widows, spinsters or deserted wives, earning a living as an alehouse keeper was a means of avoiding destitution. Ale was drunk from earthernware pots and later drinking vessels were made of wood, treated with pitch inside and had leather thong handles and called blackjacks. These pots held a pint or a quart and were replaced in the 15th century with those made of pewter and by the 1800s vessels made of glass had been introduced giving measures of a half pint and one pint.

A development from these alehouse huts were brick or stone buildings on the main routes into a town or village and known as beerhouses. Aylsham had at least five, although by the late 1800s most were termed public houses. From 1500-1660, beerhouses varied in size, some had a parlour and hall used as drinking areas, a cellar and a brewhouse. Others had a room behind a shop, or a room with family quarters on the other side or at the rear. These public drinking areas had open fires where some visitors could sit on benches in the chimney corner and others sat on stools beside trestle tables. Larger establishments had rooms on the first floor and in attics and became known as inns.

In the middle ages, the term inn was applied to private residences.

London's Inns of Court, such as Gray's Inn, Lincoln's Inn, Middle and Lower Temple are relics of a time when these places accomodated students. The Paston family of Norfolk owned a house in Norwich in the 15th century called Le Prince Inne. The inns established on main roads, offered food, liquid refreshments and accomodation where the wealthier guests could have a bedroom to themselves. The less fortunate shared a room, while others slept overnight on benches or even on the floor. All inns had stables at the rear for stabling the horses of travellers.

Some inns were established near to a church and this is evident in Aylsham where a number lay in close proximity to St Michael's church. On the Sabbath, churchwardens were empowered to interrupt the drinking of local inhabitants and forcibly carry them to church. The reverse of this situation is that churchwardens were known to slip out from church and imbibe while the sermon, which often lasted an hour or more, was being preached.

Taverns provided ale, wine and food and limited accomodation. In the 1700s, they had a clientele of the gentry, merchants, lawyers, doctors and others of affluence. These taverns, particularly in London, had a reputation of being the venues of thieves, gamblers and confidence tricksters who relieved travellers of their money and valuables.

Many public houses were purpose built or converted from former inns. These buildings had various rooms and one, the public bar, was mainly used by workmen. Others were the snug and smoke room, a lounge bar or saloon bar and at a later date, some had a ladies only bar. The different rooms tended to separate the social classes and in the Victorian era, women were actively discouraged from visiting these places and were considered to be of doubtful character should they enter this male domain.

All establishments that sold alcoholic beverages had to be licensed and from the 16th century licensing was the responsibility of the local Justices of the Peace, who were residents of local standing. These Justices had considerable judicial and administrative powers invested in them by the Crown. Further laws were enacted during the years 1751-1753 to prevent beer, wines and spirits being sold in unlicenced premises. An annual licence was made statutory and those who made an application for the first time, had to produce a character reference from a clergyman. Alehouse or beerhouse keepers were kept under close scrutiny once they were licensed and the unlicensed ones were fined every month until they were forced to close the premises.

An edict, produced in the reign of James I, laid down rules and regulations to be observed by innkeepers and guests. An act passed in 1606, placed restrictions on the buying and selling of ale and beer. This act allowed a traveller to obtain drinks during hours forbidden to local residents, and resulted in many travelling to the next village in order to continue their drinking.

The Vintners Company was incorporated by charter in 1437 and was originally called the Merchant Wine-Tonners of Gascoyne. It had two functions, the first to exercise powers over the imports and sale of wines and the second to licence premises for the sale of wines. In Aylsham, wines and spirits were available to residents from the 1500s, these were mainly imported from Europe and which only the wealthier could afford. Elizabeth I needed money to finance the war against Spain, and a tax on victuallers' licences was introduced in March 1580. Since that date, all alcoholic products have been taxed to bring in revenue to the treasury of succeeding governments.

The 19th century produced acts of parliament which affected licensing and the permitted hours of opening to the public. These measures were an attempt to curb drunkeness, and resulted in Temperance Societies being formed. The Temperance movement had the support of various religious denominations and others in society who were concerned at the poverty inflicated on women and children when the family breadwinner spent the most of his weekly wage on alcohol in the nearest inn or public house. Many individuals were persuaded to sign a pledge of abstinence. New laws for closing licensed premises on a Sunday came into effect and by 1923, it was illegal for anyone under the age of eighteen to consume an alcoholic drink in these establishments.

Social changes in recent years have enabled present day families to visit an inn or public house for lunch and most have a children's play area in the grounds. The days when many children were not allowed into licensed premises and often waited outside for long periods of time for their parents to return to them have long gone.

Within the last fifty years, a high percentage of inns and public houses have closed, particularly in rural areas. Some have been demolished and others converted into private residences. This decline coincides with the advent of stores and supermarkets where customers can buy beer, lager, wine and spirits for home consumption. Alsham is one small town where this type of shopping has undoubtedly resulted in the closure of many inns and public houses.

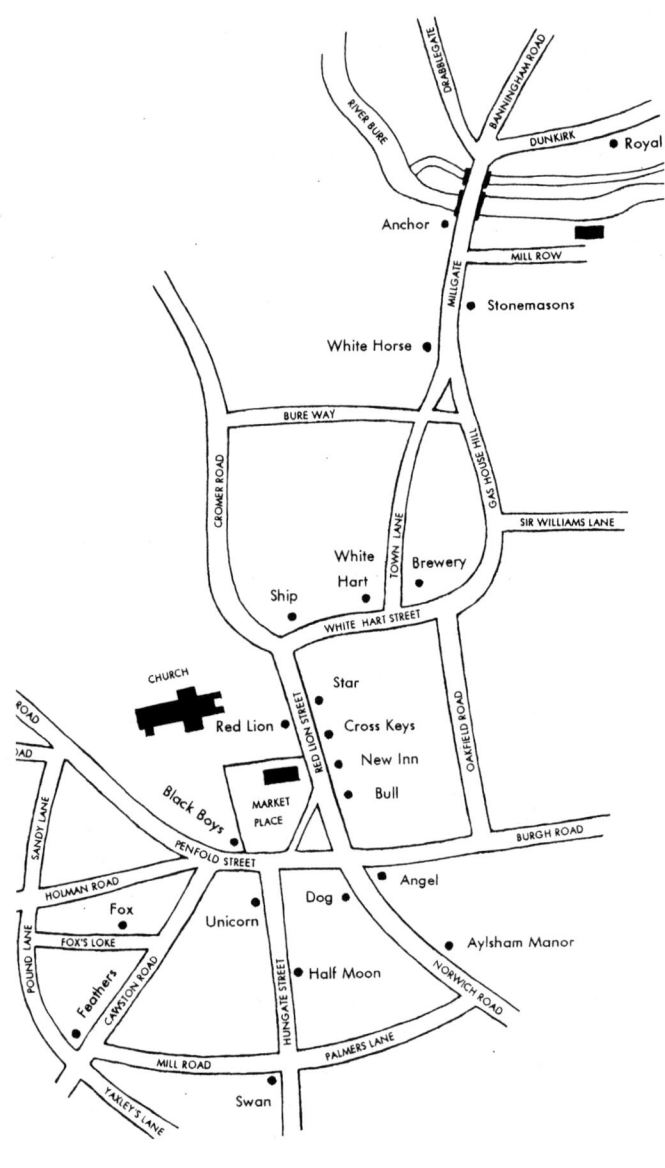

THE BLACK BOYS

PUBLICAN		OWNER	
Richard Andrews	1656	Richard & Margaret Andrews	1656
William Whittacre	1656-1667	William & Elizabeth Whittacre	1656-1667
Thomas Bell	1691-1694	Edward Edwards	1667-1670
Thomas Ward	1705-1709	John & Rose Seabourne	1670-1689
John Bray	1732-1749	Simon Ollyett	1689-1705
Francis Mosey	1749-1765	Thomas Ward	1705-1709
Richard Harriman	1765-1812	Henry Rippingall	1709-1729
Samuel & Anne Bircham	1814-1822	Thomas Bird	1729
John Secker	1822	Samuel & Anne Bircham	1814-1843
Charles Cook Tucker	1830-1836	Richard Clarke	1843-1850
Charles Tattam	1836-1843	John Secker Clarke	1870
James Spanton	1844-1854	John Secker Clarke Excrs.	1874
James Breese	1858-1864	Frederick Bullard	1874-1895
Henry Garner	1865-1874	Bullard & Sons Ltd.	1895-1967
Christmas Stapleton	1877-1904	Watney Mann (East Anglia) Ltd.	
William Pashley	1907-1909		1967-1991
Ernest Pashley	1912		
Lewis James Cope	1916-1922		
Edward Garrett	1922-1926	Inntepreneur Pub Comany	1991-1997
Daisy Garrett	1923-1926	1406 Pub Company	1997
Captain Richard Beard	1926-1930	Paula & Graham Whitehouse	1999
E.J. Neale	1930-1933		
D.J. Gathercole	1934		
Alice Emma Gathercole	1935-1957		
Francis C. Clarke	1957-1979		
Stephen Rowlands	1979-1981		
John & Jenny Ball	1981-1986		
Leah Lloyd	1992-1995		
Kevin Perry	1995-1996		
Paula & Graham Whitehouse	1996		

The Black Boys is still operating as a public house and hotel

The site of the present Black Boys was described in 1471 as a messuage and a cottage called the stonenhus in Aylsham Market Place and in 1551, the cottage was termed as le stonhouse. It is recorded in the Manor of Aylsham Lancaster Court Book that on the 21st December 1588, Rachel Norgate owned a messuage called Boy containing 6 spaces, 20 perches and le yard in the Market Place of Aylsham and which she left in her will to her two sons, Robert and William.

The Aylsham Lancaster Manor Book also records that on the 1st August 1653, Thomas Lombe and his wife Philippa, surrendered to Richard Andrews and his wife Margaret, a built up messuage on the west side of the Market Place. It was sometime William Fylt's and a cottage called 'the stonehowse' with outhouses and yards belonging to them. Although there is no definite proof, it would appear that Richard Andrews developed an inn from the messuage and cottage. He is said to have been fatally wounded by one of Oliver Cromwell's men, who were stationed at the inn. At his own request, he was buried in the grounds and his ghost is supposed to have been seen on many occasions within the building. His daughter and heir Sarah, did not retain the Black Boys. On the 20th May 1656, William Whittacre and his wife Elizabeth, obtained the ownership of a messuage and cottage called the stonehouse with adjoining outhouses and yards, now called the Black Boy. By 1659, the property was called 'The Blackboyes' and William Whittacre and his wife paid an annuity to secure it on the 29th March 1659. William Whittacre is recorded as having paid the mortgage on 'Les Blackboies' on the 2nd October 1666.

In the following year, 1667, William Whittacre mortgaged this property to Edward Edwards, a carpenter of King's Lynn and on the 4th October 1670, it passed to John Seabourne, a bookseller of King's Lynn, and his wife Rose. The ownership changed again on the 1st October 1689, when Simon Ollyett, yeoman was admitted to the Black Boys. In some documents the surname of Simon is spelled as Olliet and in a list of the churchwardens of St Michael's church, a Symond Ollyett is listed for 1693. The owners and the publicans of the Black Boys since the late 1600s has been listed, but nothing is known of the activities that took place within this inn until the early 1700s.

For the year 1710, the following was reported:-
'Public meetings of parishioners were held in the vestry of the church (St Michael's) to elect churchwardens, sidesmen and other parish officers. Nominations were made for the overseers of the poor and the surveyors of highways'.
After the business was taken care of, it was the custom to retire to the Black Boys for liquid refreshments paid for by the parish. This arrangement ended in 1821.

Daniel Defoe in 1732, recorded that in his travels in Norfolk, he found Aylsham a lively town. He records that he dined at the Three Black Boyes Inn and enjoyed a meal of rabbit pie, meat from a hock of pork, roasted goose with batter pudding and sliced potatoes with a pastry covering. Another who dined at the Black Boys was Parson Woodeforde in 1781, but he did not enjoy his meal as Daniel Defoe had done. His diary entry for the 24th September notes he and his man Will Coleman rode out from Weston at 8 a.m. and arrived in Aylsham at about 10 a.m. They put up their horses at the Black Boys and Parson Woodeforde sent for a barber, dressed himself in gown, cassock and scarf and at 11 o'clock went to the church of St Michael where he delivered a sermon. After the service, he returned to the Black Boys for dinner which consisted of boiled rump of beef, a roasted loin of veal, three roasted fowl and a ham with plain puddings. It was in his opinion a shabby overdone dinner, with the plates, knives and forks very shabby indeed.

A Miss Beauchamp Proctor visited Aylsham on Sunday 8th July 1764 and wrote in her diary:-
'We set out from Langley at eleven, Mrs Tyson, Mrs Barton, myself and maid in the coach and six. Mr Barton and Sir William in the post chaise. We dined at the King's Head at Norwich and also drank tea there. Arrived at the Black Boys at Aylsham about eight. The country between this place and Norwich is very beautiful and the road very good. We see Mr Warne's and Mr Marsham's at a distance on our right. Mr Warne's is a good looking house, something like Langley without the turrets. Mr Marsham's is a very old place smothered in trees. We lay this night at Aylsham, the beds tolerable, the house very reasonable. The town is neat and clean, it being Sunday, I could not find out their trade, but fear the undertakers have great business as there are two very smart ones living opposite one another. While our supper was preparing we took a walk and stumbled on a house, which the late Lord Townsend had begun for his mistress, but dying soon after tis left unfinished and I find is to be sold. It promises to be a very good house and is pleasantly situated'.

Cock fighting took place at the Black Boys in the 1700s and had probably taken place in previous years. Advertisements from the *Norfolk Chronicle* and the *Norwich Gazette* give the following:- 1779 'Cocking on Monday and Tuesday next (15th and 16th March) will be fought at the Black Boys in this town, a regular match between the Gentlemen of Suffolk and Aylsham consisting of twenty five main battles for five guineas each and fifty the odd. Likewise ten bye battles for two guineas each, there will be two pitts each day. Good ordinaries at the above'.
1784 'Cocking at the Black Boys in Aylsham, Norfolk on Thursday 16th and Saturday the 18th of this instant April between the

Gentlemen of Suffolk shewing thirty five mains, and ten byes; for two guineas the odd battle. Where all Gentlemen shall meet with civil usage and a hearty welcome, your humble servant, Richard Harriman'.

The Aylsham Association was formed on the 7th December 1786 at the Black Boys. The aim of this association was to protect local residents and their property from crime. There were forty one original subscribers and meetings were held annually on the first Monday in January. With the development of a small police force in Aylsham, the role of the association changed. This association is still in existence, but no longer meets at the Black Boys. It's present role is concerned with ensuring the conservation of historic Aylsham buildings and in the 1970s, the association commissioned a photographic record to be made of these buildings.

One visitor to Aylsham was Horatio Nelson, who as a young man spent his time between ships with his father at Burnham Thorpe. His cousin the Rev. Benjamin Suckling and his brother Horace lived in Aylsham at one time. The drive from Burnham Thorpe to Aylsham by coach and horses was thirty miles and Nelson stayed either with his brother or with his cousin on his visits. During the period of 1791, he passed the time as befitted a country gentleman and is said to have attended the balls known as the Aylsham Assemblies in the Assembly Room of the Black Boys.

In 1814, to celebrate the proclamation of peace after the Napoleonic wars, Samuel and Anne Bircham held a ball at the Black Boys for 200 Aylsham residents. On the 23rd June 1897, Aylsham celebrated the Diamond Jubilee of Queen Victoria with a dinner for 1800 people in the Market Place where 60 tables were erected to seat 30 persons at each table. Of the inhabitants, 750 children and old people received a free meal and others bought tickets. All the shops in the Market Place decorated their frontages with flags and bunting. The balcony of the Black Boys displayed flags and coloured bunting with a sign VR in large letters.

James Spanton, formerly of the Greyhound Inn in Norwich, took over the Black Boys in 1844 and sold the entire contents by auction. This sale took place on the 18th and 19th of April 1844 and a catalogue details the china, glassware, linen, bedding, beds and a variety of furniture and sundries to be sold. In addition a post chaise, post chariot, a gig and six horses were also offered for sale. A catalogue of this auction is in the Aylsham Archives and is unfortunately too long to be reproduced, but the first page gives the reason for James Spanton selling the entire contents of the inn. He states that he is about to refurnish the inn for the especial accomodation of the nobility, gentry, and commercial gentlemen who may honour him with their patronage. This catalogue is of interest as it gives information about the number of rooms and outbuildings at the Black Boys in 1844 and is as follows:-

Assembly Room	Kitchen	Ten bedrooms including 1 attic
Dining Room	Bar	3 Passages
Two Sitting Rooms	Larder	Staircase
Magistrates Room	Cellar	Balcony
Commercial Room	Tap Room	Landing
Maid Servants Room	Boot House	Wash House
Post Lads Room	Outside Larder	Yard
Porter Room	Mangle Room	

Before the Town Hall was built in 1857 with additions added in 1892, the Black Boys was the venue for social occasions and the meetings of various societies. Magistrates met there in the 1800's and dispensed justice. The trustees of the Norwich to Cromer Turnpike had meetings at the Black Boys from October 1815 until May 1877. Later the Inland Revenue was based there to deal with the taxes of residents.

The *Aylsham and District Almanack* for April 1903 reported to its readers:-
'The town this month was honoured by a visit from Princess Victoria. The Princess, who was accompanied by three or four friends, cycled from Overstrand, where she was staying with Lord Hillingdon. Mr C. Stapleton provided luncheon for the party at the Black Boys Hotel and before departing, the Princess took some views of the Market Place'.
In June of the same year, the *Almanack* reports:-
'Preparations had been made in Aylsham for a presentation on the 17th June of a special gift to all the children of the National Schools marking the Coronation of Edward VII. A decorated stand had been placed in the Market Place in readiness and the town band had been

engaged to march the children to the Market Place and church bells were to have been rung. Word reached the town that the King was ill and Christmas Stapleton, landlord of the Black Boys, who was to present the gifts, deemed it expedient to postpone the event. The vicar held a short service of prayers for His Majesty at the church'.

Christmas Stapleton was the publican of the Black Boys for at least twenty seven years. During this time, he actively took part in all the social occasions and festival events in Aylsham. He was from all accounts an astute business man, buying property and selling it later at a profit. One of his business enterprises was to establish his own horse drawn coaches. These were used to transport passengers from the Black Boys to Norwich and provide return journeys from the Duke's Palace to Aylsham. In 1904, Christmas Stapleton retired from the Black Boys and died in May 1912.

Early 1900s photographs show that the Black Boys had an entrance beneath a centrally placed balcony on the first floor. This entrance was a passageway leading directly into a yard at the rear where stables were provided for forty horses, attended by three ostlers. In the days when coaches and horses were the main form of transport, the Black Boys stables allowed for a change of horses on a long journey. These coaches were the Royal Mail and others transporting travellers from

Advert for the Black Boys 1880.
(Copyright Aylsham Town Council)

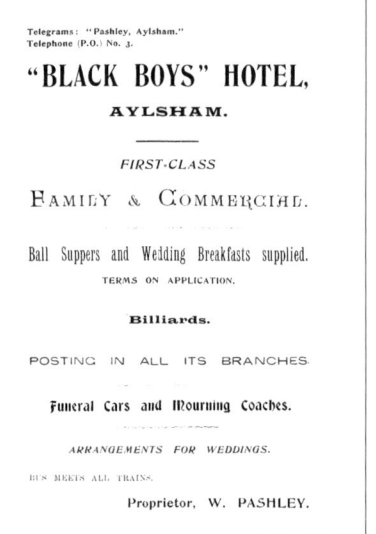

Advert for the Black Boys 1909.
(Copyright Aylsham Town Council)

Cromer to Norwich and on a return journey from Norwich to Cromer. A driver of one of these coaches was William Frederick Windham, known as 'Mad Windham' who in 1861, at the age of twenty one years, inherited the Felbrigg Hall estate. After a disastrous marriage, he incurred heavy debts, lost everything and died in poverty in 1866.

The archway at the Black Boys was filled in sometime between 1928 and 1930 and follows the semi-circular contour of the balcony. This infill became a saloon bar, with a decorative stained glass door, but is now no longer a separate bar. Information for the period 1926-1930 has been obtained from the late Margaret Beard. Her father, Captain Beard was the publican during those years and she recalls that at this time the large Assembly Room on the first floor was used every Christmas for a Masonic dinner for 100 guests. Mrs Beard did the cooking for this event, and cooked turkeys and pheasants in a large kitchen range and in two wall ovens in an extension room beyond. Fires were lighted in an outhouse underneath two or three big coppers in which puddings were boiled. The kitchen was situated at the rear of the building with windows overlooking Penfold Street. Produce for the catering was purchased from local farmers, vegetables from Market Place stalls, fish from coastal fishermen who transported their catch to Aylsham and meat and grocery provisions were

Advert for the Black Boys 1923.
(Copyright Aylsham Town Council)

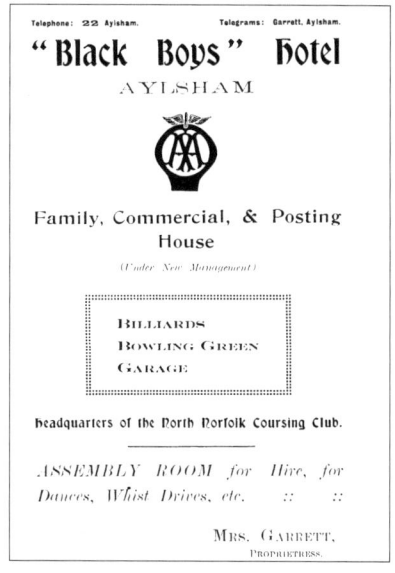

Advert for the Black Boys 1923.
(Copyright Aylsham Town Council)

supplied by the Co-Operative Society in Penfold Street.

The fruit used for puddings came from a garden and orchard belonging to the Black Boys in Cawston Road. Adjacent to these was the Black Boys bowling green, the venue for matches between other local inns and public houses. These sites, situated between the present Holman Road and Cawston Road, were later built upon with a cinema and the Aylsham Fire Brigade Station. The cinema built in 1937, closed in 1960 and became a youth centre while the fire brigade station remains to this present day.

During this period of 1926-1930 at the Black Boys, two resident maids were employed, a waitress and a barmaid for the saloon bar and two barmen in the public bar. The two maids, who were sisters, shared an attic bedroom and the two barmen were accommodated in another attic bedroom, while the barmaid occupied a bedroom on the floor below. One bedroom on the first floor was occupied by Captain Beard and his wife who shared this room with their youngest daughter until she died at the age of fourteen months. Their older daughter Margaret, had her own room on this floor and the remaining bedrooms were reserved for guests who shared a bathroom with the publican's family.

In World War I and World War II, the Black Boys was popular with servicemen stationed in Aylsham and in the surrounding areas, but shortages of beer in the latter war meant that for a few days at a time, the establishment had to be closed. When VE day was declared in 1945, the Black Boys opened its doors and the residents and servicemen celebrated in the Market Place with dancing through the front to the back of the building and out again.

Many rumours exist as to how the Black Boys acquired the name. One is that it was named after Charles II who had black hair and a swarthy complexion and was nicknamed 'The Black Boy'. The other theory is that the name originated from young black slaves who were brought to England in the 17th century as servants in wealthy Norfolk houses. As has been shown the term Boy was used in 1588 before the inn was established and later this property was referred to as Black Boy, Blackboyes, Les Blackboies and the Three Black Boys. In 1815, John Crome, an artist of the Norwich School of Painters, was commissioned to paint a sign for the inn and was obviously influenced by the Charles II theory for he chose to paint a portrait of the King.

This sign was hung from the side of the building and projected across Penfold Street, it disappeared later and no trace of it has been found. The Black Boys, originally called an inn, later became known as an hotel and is once again named as an inn. It has been listed as Grade II and is described as colourwashed brick with a black glazed pantile roof, hipped on the south side and two storeys in height with sashed windows and an attic above with dormer windows. The balcony is described as having railings flanked by Ionic pilasters and beneath the eaves, coved plaster work. This plaster work consists of three cupid like figures at the centre above the main entrance, birds resembling ravens, grapes and leaves. In recent years these have been sparsely painted in colours of black, green and yellow. In the modernisation of the interior that took place in the mid-1950s, many historic artefacts were removed, but luckily the Jacobean staircase has remained. The Black Boys Assembly Room was acquired by G. A. Key, auctioneers, surveyors and estate agents, whose business is next door and it was converted into office accomodation in 1984. The minstrels gallery has been filled in, two original fireplaces still remain and above a false ceiling, the chandeliers used to light the room are still in place.

Window from the Black Boys, date unknown
(By permission of T. W. Bishop)

21

The Black Boys 1928

The Black Boys 2001

THE UNICORN

PUBLICAN		OWNER	
Edward Rumbell			
(also listed at the Maid's Head)	1689		
John Berry	1694		
William Rising	1722-1723		
Matthew Coulfont Chalker	1723		
Robert Cubitt	1748		
Widow Cubitt	1749		
John Gilderstone	1750-1754		
Elizabeth Chalker	1755-1762		
James Wymark	1763-1777		
John De Cole	1777-1785		
Philip Heaton	1786-1792		
Edward Rice Wade	1793-1804		
Theopholis Wells	1830		
William Newstead	1843		
Phillis. Newstead	1843	Robert Hawes	1836-1841
Peter Pike	1845-1850		
William Puncher	1850-1854		
William Hill	1856-1858		
George Wells	1863-1875	John Bolding	1863-1893
Walter Whiley	1877-1893	Steward & Patteson	1893-1960
James Beck	1896-1900		
Edward Charles Balls			
+ fishmonger	1904-1930		
Harry Balls	1930-1931		
Noah Claxton	1931-1933		
Donald Wilfred Gordon Want	1937		
? Anderson	1949	Watney's Brewery	1960
Edwin and Naida Laxen	1949-1972	Norwich Brewery	1984-1995
Ted and June Bedder	1972-1986		
Ian Skelton	1986-1995		
Peter and Paula Farrand	1995	Intrepreneur Pub Company Ltd.	1995
		Spring Inns	1997

The Unicorn is still operating as a public house.

In medieval times, Hungate Street was one of the main routes into Aylsham and the Unicorn was built on this thoroughfare in the 1600s. It was a small timber framed rectangular building on two floors with small windows and a thatched roof, but in later years extensions were added and the thatched roof was replaced with pantiles. A lean-to construction was added to the front as a kitchen and storage area and cottages, which were close to the inn on the left hand side, have been incorporated to form one long bar on the ground floor and further rooms on the upper floor.

The layout of the early interior is unknown, but there is information from the late 1940s. In 1949, the ground floor had a main bar with a small counter, a smoking room and a dining room for guests. This floor also provided private rooms for the publican with a kitchen, sitting room and a living room with a filled in and long disused well beneath the floor. Stairs led from the main dining room to four bedrooms on the first floor and a bathroom and toilet, which were shared by guests and the publican's family. Customers who visited the bars had to use a toilet in the yard. All the public and private rooms were heated by log or coal fires.

The main bar had wrought iron tables and chairs on a wood floor which was oiled once a year and the smoking room was furnished with small tables and wooden benches on a linolium covered floor. Beneath the ground floor, a cellar extended for thirty feet and was divided into three sections to accomodate beer barrels, bottled beers, wines and spirits. Once a week, the beer barrels were delivered by draymen from the Steward & Patteson Brewery, stacked on trestles in the cellar, where they were tapped and pumps delivered the beer to the bar above.

By the late 1950s, those who stayed at the inn were mainly holiday makers, who came for bed and breakfast; others catered for were coach parties on sight seeing tours to Aylsham. Many lunch time patrons could obtain simple fare to accompany their liquid refreshments and regular customers whether they came at mid-day or in the evening were able to enjoy games of dominoes, darts or crib. The inn was the first in Aylsham to instal a juke box, one arm bandit and pin ball machines for the enjoyment of patrons. Apart from paying guests, and regular customers, the inn was also used for the monthly meetings of the Farmer's Union and the Angling and Rifle Clubs.

The Unicorn had a bowling green, situated to the left of the front of the building, and this had no doubt been in existence from the early days. The game of bowls was a popular past-time and James Beck, the publican from 1896-1900 advertised in the '*Aylsham and North Walsham Almanack*' in 1896:- 'Play commences Tuesdays and Thursdays to September 1st. Matches may be arranged with players of other parishes.' Between the inn and the bowling green, a lane led to an area of land called the Buttlands which in the 1300s was used as a practice area for archery, but fell into disuse in the sixteenth century. Part of this area has now been grassed over and the remainder

The Unicorn Bowling Team 1907
(By permission of Marilyn Laxen)

has been converted into a car park with access and exit from Mill Road. In the late 1980s the bowling green was sold. Two houses have been erected upon the site, and the former adjacent Unicorn stable building became an antique furniture store.

The first cinema came to Aylsham in 1914 when a large marquee was set up on the Unicorn bowling green. This was called the 'Cinematographic Palace' and the programme consisted of a film, a serial and Pathe Gazette News; it was replaced in 1921 by the West End Cinema in Penfold Street. The West End Cinema closed in 1924 and the premises became a shop for the Norwich Co-op Society and is now Barnwell's printworks.

A few details of some of the publicans of the Unicorn have been discovered and one is James Wymark who was at the inn from 1763-1777. He died aged fifty nine on the 1st July 1785 and his widow Elizabeth remained in Aylsham after she left the Unicorn and died on the 3rd August 1797 aged seventy three years, and was buried beside her husband in St Michael's churchyard. The churchyard also yields information regarding other Unicorn publicans and their families. One stone is inscribed, 'Sacred to the memory of William, son of William and Mary Puncher who died 1852.' William and Mary Puncher were at the Unicorn from 1850-1854. Another stone has been erected to Edward Rice Wade, the publican from 1793-1804, but the inscription has been eroded and is difficult to read, but is as follows:- 'In memory of Edward Rice Wade who departed this life ——— December 1822 aged 66 years. Also Mary his wife who departed this life the ——— September 1811 aged ——— years.

The Unicorn also had some connection to the Aylsham Religious Dissenters in 1830 and the following has been taken from the Aylsham Dissenter Meeting Houses Register.
On the twenty seventh day of April 1830, it was certified as follows;- 'We the undersigned being Protestant Dissenters require a meeting house, situate in the Unicorn Yard in the Parish of Aylsham in the County of Norfolk and may be duly registered in the Registry of the Lord Bishop of Norwich as a place for religious worship.
As witness our hands April 1830. I. King, John Frary, Edward Patten, Robert Bowers'.
It is interesting to note that one of the signatories was Robert Bowers, the grandson of Robert Dodman, the publican of the White Hart from 1781-1803 who had also requested a place of worship for Protestant Dissenters in 1796.

From 1949-1974, the publicans at the Unicorn were Edwin and Naida Laxen; and his family were descended from Richard Laxen who married Martha Howes in 1769. The Laxen family were saddle and harnessmakers and carried on a business in Aylsham Market Place for at least 100 years, while others became bakers and confectioners in Red Lion Street. Descendants of the original Richard Laxen were named after him and one became the publican of the Stonemason's Arms from 1875-1878. Another Richard Laxen who was born in Aylsham in 1887, went to Canada and was instrumental in setting up a settlement in Saskatchewan, named Aylsham.

Over the years, the interior of the Unicorn has changed with the removal of walls to provide one large bar room space with exposed brickwork, ceiling beams, a carpeted floor and individual tables and chairs. Inside toilets have been installed to replace those formerly located in the yard outside. On the first floor, the publican's family have their private accomodation consisting of a dining room/sitting room, kitchen, bathroom and four bedrooms with exposed original beams. The present Unicorn does not offer accomodation to guests and is now designated as a public house, it provides lunch time fare for Aylsham residents and visitors and on Friday and Saturday evenings customers can enjoy music provided by small groups of musicians.

In 1984, a survey of the Unicorn disclosed that the timber framed building had been extensively damaged by the larvae of the Death Watch beetle and an extensive renovation programme was carried out to save it. This preservation scheme was very expensive and involved a great deal of work and has proved to be successful in preserving this listed Grade II building. A painted sign of a Unicorn on a free standing pole situated on the front forecourt is plainly visible from the Market Place and Hungate Street. This sign may have been differently situated in the past, but it still conveys a message of hospitality to be found in one of Aylsham's long established historic buildings.

E. A. LAXEN

UNICORN INN

BED & BREAKFAST

AND FULLY LICENSED

HUNGATE STREET
AYLSHAM — NORFOLK

Advert for The Unicorn 1968.
(Copyright Aylsham Town Council)

The Unicorn 1964, Edwin Laxen on the far left.
(By permission of Marilyn Laxen)

The Unicorn 2001.

THE HALF MOON INN

The Half Moon Inn was located at what is now known as Half Moon Cottage, 19 Hungate Street. The earliest reference to this inn is in 1700 when Thomas Bell was the publican and possibly the owner. It was acquired by Henry Wymark in 1720 and his son James inherited the property and sold it in 1748 to Benjamin Wiggott. The inn closed in that year and the premises were converted into a bakery.

On the 22nd October 1750, Henry and Hannah Savory purchased the Half Moon property, but it would appear that this was not an outright purchase as they obtained a loan from Robert Parmeter. The residue of this loan was paid in 1765. By 1768, Ursula Greenwood, a widow, was the owner and it was listed at that time as a dwelling house, brewhouse and bakehouse. The mention of the brewhouse is evidence that in the past, beer had been brewed on the premises. Ursula Greenwood sold the property to Joseph Sexton in 1768. By 1827 he had died and his son, also called Joseph, had inherited. The James Wright map of 1839 shows that Joseph Sexton II owned and occupied a house, buildings and yards. After the death of Joseph Sexton II in 1879, the Half Moon bakery was purchased by a miller, Henry Gardener Hart. He and his wife Mary Ann sold the lease to Robert Manthorpe of Cawston. At this time the premises were occupied by Thomas Howe, a baker and corn chandler, who remained there until 1892.

In 1889, Robert Manthorpe, sold the Half Moon bakery to Morgan's Brewery. This brewery company supported the bakery and used it as an outlet for their bottled beers; it was leased to John Postle in 1900. John Postle was succeeded by his son Ernest in 1908 who continued until his retirement in 1937. The bakery continued under the direction of the Postle family until 1959 when it closed.

A document, dated 14th October 1960, lists 19 Hungate Street as the former Half Moon Inn and bakery, a freehold property for sale by Morgan's Brewery Company Ltd. This is as follows:-
'By Conveyance so dated and made between Morgan's Brewery Company Ltd. (the Vendor) of the one part and Christopher George Wilmot Jackson, farmer of Church Cottage, Shotesham, Norfolk (the Puchaser) of the other part
1) The Vendor as Beneficial Owner thereby conveyed unto the Purchaser. All that piece or parcel of land situate at Hungate Street, Aylsham, in the County of Norfolk together with the dwellinghouse,

shop and premises erected thereon or on some part thereof formerly known as the 'Half Moon', but then known as 19 Hungate Street, Aylsham aforesaid'.

Since 1961, the former Half Moon has passed to various owners and although this building is now a private residence, it has retained many original features from the time when it was an inn.

The former Half Moon Inn.

THE SWAN

PUBLICAN

Anne Maires	1620
Edward Pinchin	1689
Fiddy Barnes	1731-1733
James Dadley	1837-1843
George Greengrass	1853
Allen Pye	1856
John Watson	1864-1865
Dennis Shaw + shoemaker	1868-1869
Maria Cooke	1874-1883
William Cooke	1891-1900
Leonard G Page	1925-1933
Mrs G. Page	1933-1969

OWNER

Robert Beasy	1837
William Bircham	1839
William Bircham & Co.	1864-1874
Steward & Patteson	1878-1893

The Swan was demolished in 1969

The Swan was an inn in 1620, but by the 1900s it had ceased to be in this category and had become known as a public house. It was situated on the west corner of Mill Road and the junction of Hungate Street and was of a substantial size. Unfortunately it has been impossible to discover any information of the publicans and owners between 1733 and 1837.

The inn was owned by Robert Beasy in 1837, a man of some financial means, who had built thirteen dwellings with yards to the west of the Swan. These were known as Beasy's Rookery and he let them to tenants, the poorest of Aylsham residents, who brought up large families in cramped conditions. Robert Beasy occupied a residence nearby and employed a publican to carry on the day to day running of his inn.

By 1839, the Swan had been purchased by William Bircham, the Reepham brewer and at this time it was described as a red brick building with a pantile roof, two storeys in height with attic rooms above. Later information describes it as having an entrance through a door in Mill Lane, later named Mill Road, with steps down to two bars. One of these bars in the late 1800s was the Smoke Room and the other a Public Bar and both of these had wooden benches and separate tables, and beer at this time was served from barrels which were brought up from an underground cellar. In a yard outside there was a skittle ground, outbuildings, a garden and a well with ropes, buckets and winding gear that supplied the inn with water.

In 1878, William Bircham & Co. sold the Swan to Messrs. Donald Steward and H.S. Patteson. These new owners continued to maintain the Swan and there is some confusion about its status as in the Norfolk Directories of this time it is referred to as a public house, therefore no longer an inn accommodating guests, and in other directories it is classified as a beerhouse. Maria Cooke was the publican in 1881 and at this time she was aged forty nine years and her fifty one year old husband, John Hannant Cooke was a tailor journeyman. They had four children, William born in 1859, Frances 1864, Ward 1876 and Thomas in 1879. William became a shoemaker journeyman and the publican of the Swan in 1891. Frances Cooke, at the age of seventeen years was a general domestic servant and Ward, at the age of fifteen years became a bricklayer's boy. By 1888, John Hannant Cook had become the publican of the Cross Keys in Red Lion Street.

The Swan was the nearest public house to the Aylsham South Railway Station and was patronised by many railway employees in their off duty hours and was the venue for many meetings of the National Union of Railwaymen. Although the Swan was a listed building of historic interest, it was demolished in 1969 and Aylsham lost one of its finest old buildings. The site of this former inn is now a car park, the grounds and Beasy's Rookery, demolished many years ago, are now built over with bungalows, named Swan Close.

The Swan 1965
(By permission of N Crick)

THE FEATHERS

PUBLICAN		OWNER
Edmund Roberts	1843	
George Lovell Thomas King	1845	
John Moy	1846-1869	
Stephen Underwood	1875	
Charles Underwood	1877	
Walter Durrell + Currier	1879-1883	Bullard & Sons 1879-1964
George Warne + grocer	1888-1910	
David and Laura Doidge	1910-1930	
Emma and Charles Hewitt	1930-1936	
Emma Hewitt	1936-1938	
Emma and Ronald Warne	1938-1967	
Trevor Gould	1967-1977	Courage
Michael Rouse	1977-1987	Interpreneur Pub Co. Ltd
Barry and Pat Waller	1987	
Michael and Helen Woolley		Phoenix
Roland and Shelley Mawston	1991-1999	Criterian Inns

The Feathers is still operating as a public house.

This public house at 54, Cawston Road is a Grade II listed building of the mid 19th century. Two storeys in height, it has small grey coastal stones covering the front facade with two sash windows on the ground floor and two above with a blind window in between. The windows and each end of the building are outlined in yellow brick and a front porch, added at a later date, is constructed in the same yellow coloured bricks.

The roof is slated grey with a chimney stack at each end, and on the right hand side there is a narrow red brick, two storey extension with a sash window on each floor. On the left, a one storey extension with a red pantile roof was added to the original main building in the late 1800s and in the early 1900s it was a grocery shop. This shop was run by the wife of the publican George Warne and her sister Harriet Doughty, who not only sold groceries, but also meat and their own make of sausages. The grocery shop closed in 1910 and the premises were taken over by George and Alan Cooper for their bicycle business. They later moved to the Bull Inn, in Red Lion Street, which had been closed in 1907. The Cooper brothers expanded their business from bicycles to the hiring and selling of motorcars, and became very successful at their new location in Red Lion Street.

In the mid-1900s, the Feathers had three separate bars leading off a central passage with the main bar on the left, the Smoke Room to the right and the Snug at the rear. These bars had flagstone floors, covered in coconut matting, wooden benches and long tables. A staircase led to a landing and six bedrooms, one of which was converted into a combined toilet and bathroom in 1937. Prior to this date, the publican's family used a toilet in the rear yard and another toilet in this area was for the use of male patrons of the public house, who were mainly agricultural workers or the residents who lived in nearby small houses and cottages.

Although the front of the Feathers was built in a decorative fashion, the rear of the building was very different in style and was constructed of red brick, with small windows and a plain back door. An entrance in Pound Lane provided access to the rear yard where beer barrels were delivered. In this yard there is a long red brick building, which in the 1800s was used as a skittle alley, but by the 1900s it was no longer used for this purpose and was converted into a store room and garage. The game of skittles, which took place in many inns and public houses of Aylsham, came to an end in the late 1800s and these games were replaced by bowling matches and darts competitions. The latter continue to this day between the remaining public houses in Aylsham.

A free standing pole on the boundary of the Feathers shows a sign of the Prince of Wales emblem as this public house was named after Edward, Prince of Wales, the eldest son of Queen Victoria who later became King Edward VII.

Although few details have emerged about some of the publicans, some facts are known. John Moy, the publican from 1846 until 1869, died in 1882 at the age of 88 years. He was buried in Aylsham Cemetary beside his wife Sarah who had died in 1876 aged 81 years. Charles Albert Hewitt, the publican in 1930, died aged 30 years in 1936. His widow Emma continued as the publican until her marriage to Ronald Warne in 1938 when they became joint publicans.

*Emma & and Ronald Warne
at the Feathers 1938.*
(by permission of Joan Ducker)

The Feathers 2001

THE DOG

PUBLICAN		OWNER	
Thomas Allen	1689		
Thomas Lubbock	1722-1730		
Thomas Clarke	1731-1733		
Francis Mosey	1736-1746		
William Raynforth	1747-1763		
John Andrews	1764-1779		
William Wetherell	1780-1782		
Robert Wetherell	1783-1789		
Widow Wetherell	1790		
Robert Dye	1790-1797	Robert Dye	1790-1797
Elizabeth Dye	1797-1806	Elizabeth Dye	1797-1806
George Back	1807		
Henry Rix	1826		
John Davey	1830		
William Cutting	1836-1843	John Youngs & William Burt	1839-1843
Richard Smith, farmer & horsedealer	1845-1846		
Peter Rix	1850		
James Ebden	1853		
Samuel Mullinger	1854		
William Puncher	1858-1872	Robert Leaman	1858
Thomas Martin Dickerson	1875-1881		
Benjamin Bowyer	1882	George R. Porret	1882-1888
Mary Bowyer	1883-1888		
C.A. Thompson	1888		
William Pashley	1890-1904	Morgan & Co.	1888-1929
Alfred Dyball	1908-1911		
George Rich	1912-1914		
Robert Francis	1916		
W.F. Hogg	1921-1923		
William Melonie	1924		
Emily Louisa Melonie	1925		
J.I. Hart-Bowgen	1926-1928		
William Crisp	1930-1932		
S.G. Scrutton	1935		
Mrs S.G. Scrutton	1936		
Alexander William Wills	1937-1939		
Mrs Wills	1939		
Tony Eggleton			
? Rabin	1951-1953		
Captain Thrower	1954-1958		
Bill Laws			
Jerry Jones			
Derek Twaite	1966		

The Dog closed in 1966

One of the earliest references to the Dog comes from the Aylsham Lancaster Court Book 1664-1704. An entry states:-
'Christopher Some, son and heir of John and Frances Some admitted to a messuage in Aylsham called 'Le Dogg' which formerly was held

by Richard Milborne then by John Some who took it up at a Court held on 9th May 1642 being inherited by will of his father George Some, Le Dogg has a barn, garden, cartshed and a pasture yard called le backyard'
This messuage was situated on the Norwich Road, near Burgh Road and opposite the Angel Inn. It may possibly have been an inn in 1642 and by 1689 was known as the Dog Inn.

An advertisement in the *Bury and Norwich Post* for Wednesday 25th August 1790 reads as follows:-
'Robert Dye respectfully acquaints the public that he has taken the DOG INN in Aylsham in the County of Norfolk, which he has fitted up and furnished with every desirable accomodation and stored his cellars with the choicest wines and other liquors. He therefore, humbly solicits the favours of the former customers to the above Inn, and those of the public in general, assuring them, nothing in his power shall be wanting to merit their favours and esteem'.
A description of the Dog in 1797 gives the following information:-
'It has its own brewhouse, a bowling green, two dining rooms, one 31ft. by 22ft. and the other 15ft. by 15ft. There are three parlours, five chambers and attic rooms'.

The *Aylsham Illustrated Almanack* for 1884 had this advertisement:-
'The DOG INN, Aylsham. Commercial and Family Establishment. Mrs Bowyer, Proprietress.
Mrs Bowyer, in soliciting a share of Public Patronage, begs to state that every attention will be given to the comfort of Commercial and Railway Travellers and the Public generally. Good beds, refreshments of first class quality and charges reasonable. Estimates given to Excursionists for Breakfast, Dinners and Teas on application'.
The same publication in 1888 produced another advertisement.
'DOG Commercial Inn, Aylsham. C. A. Thompson, Proprietor.
Morgan & Co's Celebrated Ales and Stout on draught. Wines and Spirits of the very best quality. Allsopp's, Aitchison's and Bass Ales, Guiness Dublin Stout. Moderate charges'.

An advertisement in the *Norwich Mercury* for Saturday 19th January 1850 is as follows:-
'DOG INN, Aylsham.
Peter Rix, late of Swanton Morley, having taken the above inn, most respectfully informs the Nobility, Gentry, and the Public in general,

that he has laid in a stock of the Best Wines and Spiritous Liquors, and London Porter, hoping by strict attention the merit of their patronage and support.
N.B. Good accomodation for Commercial Travellers etc,. Neat Post Chaise and Gigs, with good Horses and Careful Drivers, on the shortest notice'.

A sale catalogue in the Aylsham Archives shows that on the 11th December 1855, the Dog Inn was offered for sale to speculative builders and others by Mr Butcher, an auctioneer. The property was divided into five lots, which could be bought in separate units or as one whole unit. It was however purchased as a whole and this enabled the inn to continue for another one hundred and eleven years. This catalogue for the sale is of interest as it provides details of the Dog as it was at that time and is quoted below.

LOT I
The North Part of the House Premises and Stables, called 'The Dog Inn' consisting of an Entrance Passage, a Parlour called the Coach Room, Kitchen, Bar, Wash House and Larder, with a good Wine and Spirit Cellar under; and five Bed-Rooms, Attics over the same. A small Back Yard, in which are Fowls Houses, Firing Shed etc. A Capital Stable containing five Stalls and two Loose Boxes, with open Standing for Carriages; and part of the large Yard in front thereof (as staked out and shown on the Plan) This lot has a frontage of 28ft. 9ins. next the Turnpike Road to Norwich and Cromer.
LOT II
Comprises the principal Entrance to 'The Dog Inn' a comfortable Commercial Room and Porter Room, with a good Beer Cellar; a Staircase, Landing and Water Closet, and an Upper Sitting Room, and Bed-Room; with Attics over. Also two spacious Coach Houses, or Stables, with Hay Chamber over the same, and part of the large Yard adjoining with Pump thereon, and Entrance at the South End of Lot 3. This lot has frontage of 32ft. 8ins. next the said Turnpike Road.
LOT III
Consists of the Large Room, called 'The Court Room' used for Assemblies etc. 34ft. by 25ft. with attics over; and two Stables of four Stalls and three Stalls under. Also Part of the large Yard adjoining (as staked out and shown on the Plan) This Lot has a frontage of 33 feet next the said Turnpike Road.

LOT IV
Comprises an excellent Six Stall Stable and Four Stall Stable with Hay Chamber, a Lean-to-Loose box opening into a small Yard and Part of the large Yard in front of the Stables (as staked out and shown on the Plan).

LOT V
Consists of the valuable Piece of Land used as a Bowling Green, with Summer Houses and a small Bar Room standing thereon; a strip of the large Yard adjoining Lots 2 and 4 (as staked out and shown on the Plan); and a Piece of Land next the Turnpike Road used as a Horse Yard; the whole containing about 55 Roods, having a frontage of 102 ft. 6ins. next the said Turnpike Road and admirably adapted for Building Purposes. The entire estate is the Copyhold of the Manor of Aylsham Lancaster.

It is not known how many staff were employed at the Dog Inn, but some certainly came from the Aylsham workhouse. One, who is documented from the Admissions To The Workhouse Book for 1803-1836, is Thomas Spink, referred to as a pauper, who was admitted on the 21st October 1826 aged fourteen years. He was discharged six days later to Henry Rix, the publican of the Dog and was

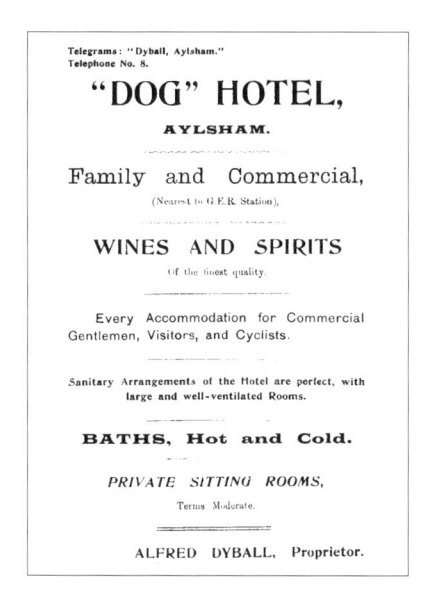

Advert for the Dog 1909.
(Copyright Aylsham Town Council)

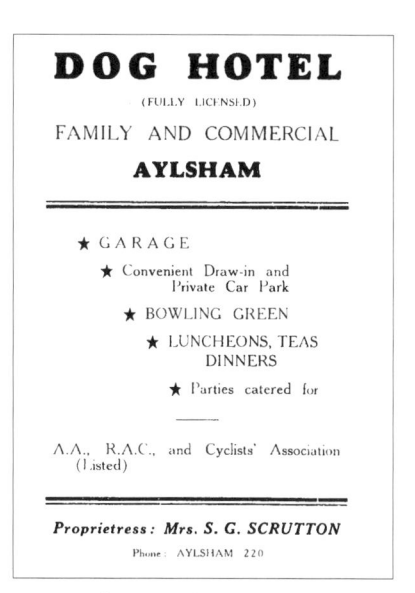

Advert for the Dog 1936.
(Copyright Aylsham Town Council)

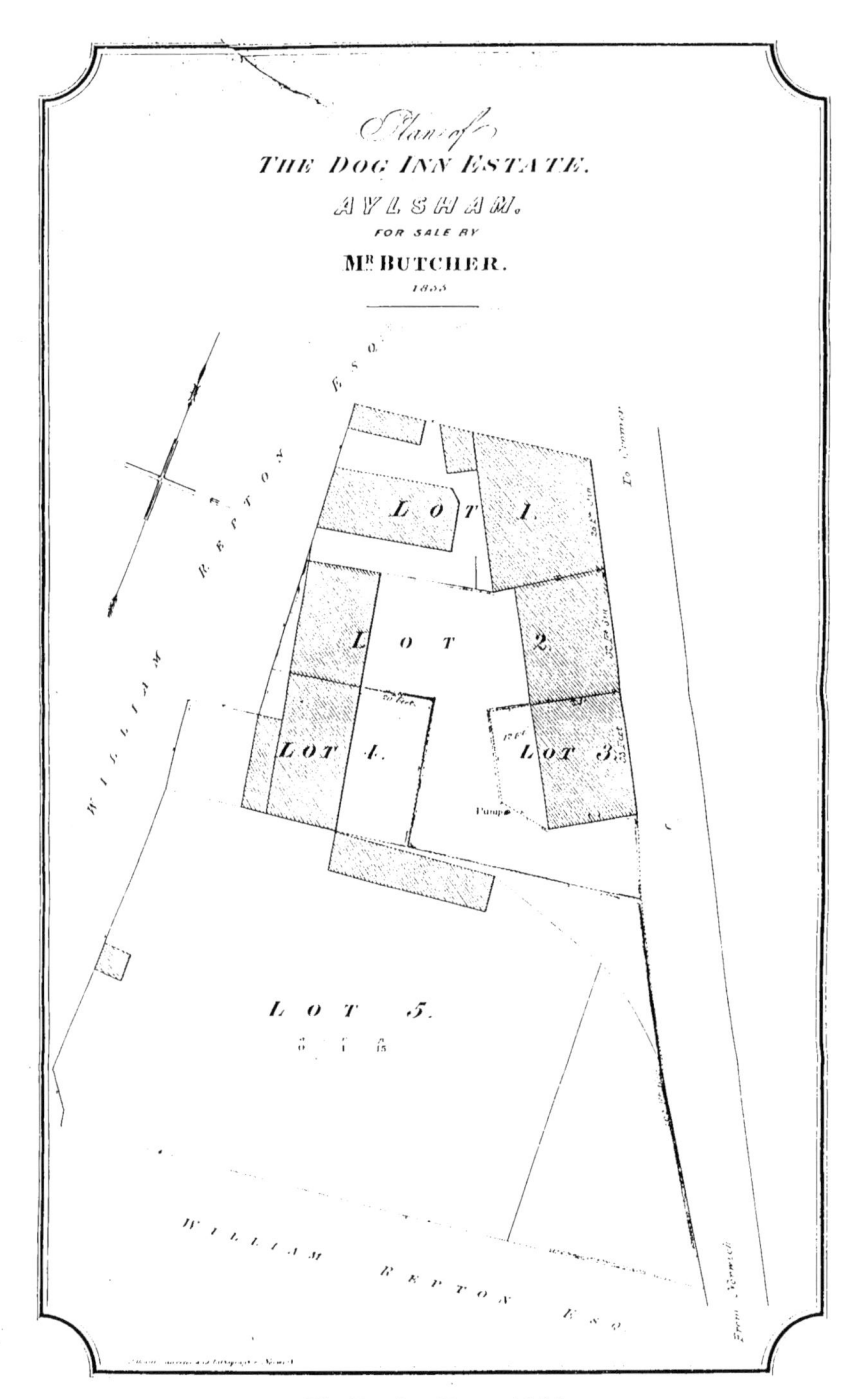

The Dog Inn Estate 1855
(Copyright Aylsham Town Council)

employed in domestic duties. In 1881, Susan Pegg, aged twenty one was employed as a general domestic servant. In the early days, the Dog was referred to as an inn and later it was termed an hotel. It was the venue for many social events and the County Court, established in 1847, sat there monthly, but later moved to the Black Boys. This court later met bi-monthly at the Town Hall after it was built in 1858. During the 1800s the Trustees of the Norwich to Cromer Turnpike and the Commissioners of the Aylsham Navigation held their meetings at the inn.

The threat of an invasion by Napoleon in 1803, prompted the formation of a Volunteer Corps and sixty one Aylsham men enrolled as 'The Loyal Aylsham Volunteers'. This company eventually disbanded, but was re-formed after 1859 as the 6th Aylsham Company. These volunteers were required to provide their own uniforms of plain grey cloth, trimmed with black braid and they drilled on the Dog bowling green. Five of these volunteers enlisted for army service in the Boer War and two privates were presented with personal uniforms at a reception held at the Dog Inn.

After the railways came to Aylsham, the Dog became known as an hotel and accommodated many travellers and some railway staff. In the freezing winter conditions of 1947, railway staff and some passengers stayed overnight at the hotel as it was impossible to move the trains from the nearby Aylsham South Station.

The Dog Hotel closed in 1966 and the site has been developed as a row of shops, a bank and a supermarket. The former bowling green is now a car park for the supermarket and all that remains is a wall that once marked the boundary of the bowling green and a house and garden in Hungate Street where James Gogle lived in 1797.

Pictured (on the opposite page) in 1900 Bowling Team at The Dog are:-

Front Row left to right:- Jack Webster, Ernest Pike, Cecil Gilbert, Ernest Pashley, Walter Wade, Robert Proudfoot, George Pike, Fred Keyner

2nd Row:- John Soame, H. J. Gidney, White Christmas Stapleton, Aldis, Harry Proudfoot, Ed Browne, Knights, Sidney Bones

3rd Row:- Seeley, Arnold Ingate, Henry Page, Ben Cook, Harry Marjaram, Elliot, S. Baker, Philip Green, E Pashley, Larke, Edward Bird, Revd. Robert Gaye, Dr. Fred Little, Edwards, Joe Keymer

Back Row:- Archie Boyd, Horace Steward, Clarke, Dester, Walter Tuttle, Albert Pumphrey, Bertie Laxen

Bowling Team at The Dog 1900
(Copyright Aylsham Town Council)

The Dog Bowling Green 1910

AYLSHAM MANOR

The Aylsham Manor in the Norwich Road is probably the oldest building of note in the town. There is evidence of it dating from 1550 and a 33 feet long oak beam in the entrance hall ceiling is in accordance with this date, but the rest of the house is of the late seventeenth and eighteenth centuries.

The Manor House was purchased by Bishop John Jegon about 1611 and it is thought that he rebuilt or enlarged parts of the house. Bishop Jegon had formerly been master of Corpus Christi College, Cambridge in 1590 and was elected Vice-Chancellor of the university from 1596-1601. He was chaplain to Queen Elizabeth I and in 1601 appointed Dean of Norwich and became a bishop in 1603. While living in Aylsham Manor, he purchased a considerable amount of land in the district. He died on the 13th March 1618 and was buried in St Michael's church in Aylsham.

Aylsham Manor has had many owners since Bishop Jegon and one was James Bulwer who owned the property in 1839. At this time it is listed as consisting of the manor house, yards, garden, lawn, plantations, barns and outbuildings. Apart from this property, James Bulwer owned other properties and land in and around Aylsham. Henry James Bowman was the owner in 1912 and he bought several acres of surrounding land. After his death, the property passed to his wife and was inherited by their two daughters, Lucy Hulbert Bowman and Veronica Duson in 1975. They sold the manor and land to Maureen and Ronald Barnes, who applied for planning permission to convert the house to licensed premises and a restaurant.

Permission was granted for this conversion, but alterations at the manor entrance from Norwich Road were required for safety reasons. The entrance and exit to the manor was through iron gates, set in an old red brick wall and close to the road, and obscured the view of any vehicles leaving the premises. The gates were removed, parts of the wall on both sides of these gates were demolished and a new entrance was made by cutting back into the drive. This new entrance provided low flower beds on each side and full visual access for drivers leaving the manor.

Extensive changes were made to the interior of the house with the hallway converted into a bar with a counter on the right hand side. A room to the right became the dining area of the restaurant with separate tables and chairs. On the left there was a function room, another room was a lounge where customers could enjoy their drinks while seated on comfortable leather sofas or armchairs. In the interior refurbishment of the Aylsham Manor to licensed premises, the oak panelling in the main rooms, which dated back to the seventeenth or eighteenth centuries, were painted over.

The Aylsham Manor opened to the public as licensed premises in November 1979 and closed eight months later in July 1980. During these few months it was a popular venue for Aylsham residents who could enjoy the facilities offered and where patrons could enjoy good food, wine and beer in the restaurant. After the closure of the manor it was purchased by Mrs & Mrs Wilmot Ching in 1981 and converted into a residential home for the elderly and has continued in this capacity. The elderly residents who take pleasure in living in this historic house, also enjoy the extensive grounds which are planted with trees, shrubs and flowers and give so much pleasure during the changing seasons.

THE ANGEL INN

The Angel Inn was located at the junction of the Norwich and Burgh Roads and dates from 1615. Built of red bricks, the end gable abuts the Norwich Road and entry to the inn was directly from this road, separated from the stable block by a cobbled yard.

An entry in the Aylsham Rental for the 29th September 1619 gives details of this property, then owned by Thomas Cressy. 'A messuage in Aylsham called Le Angell containing 10 bayes, 2 stables, 5 bayes and Le Yard and Close adjoining. Area 2 acres and 2 roods. A piece of land called le Ollands formerly Robert Clare's. Area 11 acres'.
The close referred to became known as Angel Close and was land along the Burgh Road.

It is not known when the Angel ceased to operate as an inn, but an item in the Churchwarden's Accounts dated 1637 shows that it was still an inn at that time.
'Item:- For careing the waynescott from my yard to the church and the joyners utensills from the Angell to the church 8d'.
This entry refers to St Michael's pulpit which was made from oak panelling bought in Norwich, transported to the craftsmens yards in Aylsham, cut into pieces and carved. These separate pieces were taken to the church and assembled.

Further details regarding the Angel are given in the will of Robert Hall of Aylsham made on the 22nd June 1669.
'Weak in body, Soul to God hoping for pardon of sins and everlasting life through Jesus Christ.
To son Robert, houses and lands I purchased of the Feoffees of Sir John Robert and called Kittlebridge. Also to Robert the closes containing 28 acres which I had of Mr Rossell of Norwich.
To son Richard, my several lands and enclosures which I had lately of Arthur Jegon Esq. Also to Richard the close I purchased of Tramplet, called Tramplet close, and the close I had of Robert Russell lying near Mevies (Movies?) Beck; my houses and lands called the Angel, which I had of Thomas Knolles, the houses and yards called 'the old Jayle' with my other house and yard called Wagsteres, where Swan the carpenter now dwells'.

The next date known for the Angel is 1689 when a Matthew Dye is listed as the publican. In 1729, John Bennett, who owned a great deal of property and land in Aylsham, had acquired Angel Close. An extract from his will of 1764 states:- 'I give and devise to the said Thomas Leigh Bennett, my youngest son, my copyhold messuage with the outhouses, yards, garden, the enclosure called the Angel Close whereon standeth a little barn and my 2 pightles thereto adjoining called Hovell's pightles and all now in my own use'. Thomas Leigh Bennett however, did not inherit this land and property as before his father died in 1765, he made a codicil leaving it all to his son-in-law John Wace.

The person most associated with the Angel is Thomas Cressy who owned the property in 1615. In his will dated 2nd March 1616, he left twelve tenements in Millgate for the use of the poor. These were let at a low rent, but brought in sufficient revenue for any building repairs and any surplus was given to the poor and needy of Aylsham. Thomas Cressy's will appointed some of his fellow churchwardens as the trustees of this charity. In 1776, a workhouse was built on part of this land, situated in the angle between New Road and Commercial Road (now Bure Way). The parish workhouse was demolished in 1842 and the land and materials were sold along with the cottages. The trustees invested the money that was received and the interest was given to the poor at Christmas. 'Cressy's Charity' as it was known, still exists and the money is now used for other worthwhile purposes.

Although the closure date of the Angel Inn is not known, some parts of it remain and have been incorporated into the Old Bank House, 3 Norwich Road, which was built in the early eighteenth century. The gateway entrance to the inn, where once horses, carriages and carts clattered over cobbles, has long since gone. The space has been filled with a building which is now a solicitors office. At one time this office was accessible through a door in the Old Bank House building, but this has subsequently been bricked up. The Old Bank House is so called as early in the nineteenth century, the banking business of Copeman & Co. was carried on from this address. The Copeman family had been wealthy and influential in Aylsham with some members attorneys while others were in banking. The senior partner in Copeman & Co. was Robert Copeman Junior. He was succeeded by his sons George and Thomas; the latter lived at the Old Bank House, while George lived at West Lodge. In 1815, a bank note license was issued to Copeman & Co. and they produced their own £5 notes. The bank prospered with business from landowners, farmers and shopkeepers.

By 1847, James Harrod was the Copeman's chief clerk or manager and he was later succeeded by Jacob Middleton. The bank had an alarm system in case of an attempted robbery, which was a bell on the roof with a rope going down to the bank parlour. Eight years later in 1855, Copeman's bank was purchased by Gurney and Company, a firm of Norwich bankers who continued the business in the Old Bank House for another four years when it was transferred to premises in the Market Place with Jacob Middleton as the manager. Gurney & Co. amalgamated with nineteen other private banks in 1896 to form Barclay & Co. and in 1917, the name was changed to Barclay's Bank Limited.

Following the sale of the Copeman bank, the Old Bank House was sold in 1860 to W. H. Scott, a solicitor who carried on his practice until 1882. He was succeeded by another solicitor H. J. Gidney 1882-1930 and the last solicitor to occupy the building was D. L. Walker from 1930 until his retirement. He later sold the house and it is now a private residence.

The Old Bank House, with parts of the building dating from the 1600s, is Grade II listed and lies in the conservation area of Aylsham. The interior of the house is a fascinating mixture of the centuries with exposed beams, while in some rooms in the later building there is fine eighteenth century panelling. An impressive entrance hall is the height of the two storeys and has columns supporting the original seventeenth century wall. The staircase has two turned balusters per tread, and may date from the eighteenth century.

Although the Old Bank House has had many owners over the years from when it was a small inn, they have made few changes to the interior and subsequently many original features have been preserved. Many who pass the entrance to the Old Bank House in Burgh Road will be unaware that this lovely house, with its well proportioned windows and impressive doorway, was once the site of an old inn. In addition around the corner in the Norwich Road there is a red brick two storey wall, built in the style of a Dutch gable and this was the end wall of the old Angel Inn. This wall is not the original, but was re-built in the eighteenth century.

THE BULL INN

PUBLICAN		OWNER	
Jul (?) Bowman	1700	Thomas Hall (date unknown)	
Dowing or Dewing	1721-1723	Samuel Hutchison	1669
Thomas Lack	1730-1745	Mary and Robert Vowte	1670
William Green	1746-1747		
Widow Green	1748-1755		
Thomas Hooks	1756-1774		
Mary Hooks	1775-1789		
John Burton	1789-1790		
James Levick	1791-1795		
John Secker	1795-1820		
John Puncher	1825-1830		
Benjamin Brett	1836		
John Hopkins	1839	Robert Hawes	1839
Dick Feek + horsebreaker	1843-1848		
William Purdy	1850		
Robert Rust	1853		
Robert Cossor	1854	Francis Parmeter & William Bircham	1856
Henry Williamson	1856		
John Watson	1858-1863		
Samuel Poll	1864-1865	Bircham & Son	1865
Matthew Bayfield + sheep clipper	1868-1869		
William Poll	1872-1900	Bullard & Son	1887-1907
William Joiner	1900-1907		

The Bull Inn closed in 1907

The Bull Inn was a small thatched roof building in Red Lion Street dating from the 1600s, and owned in 1669 by Samuel Hutchison. He sold it that year to Mary and Robert Vowte and it was described in the sale as a messuage called Le Bull, situated in Aylsham. This property had formerly been owned by Thomas Hall, but the dates of his ownership are unknown.

In 1795, the publican John Secker, was paid 2/- for Robert Meddler's board and lodging by the Aylsham Parish Council. The reason for this transaction has not been established, but it is likely that Robert Meddler was from the Aylsham Workhouse. Some facts are known about those who were at the Bull in the 1800s. On the 11th October 1825, Elizabeth Lovick was apprenticed to John Puncher, the publican, for a term of three years. She was sixteen years of age and her parents John and Mary Lovick, had given permission for her apprenticeship. John Puncher received £4 for Elizabeth's apprenticeship, which probably meant that she worked as a general domestic servant. Sometimes apprentices were unhappy in their placements and ran away only to be forced by the law to return.

Dick Feek, was the publican in 1843 and in 1848 had moved next door to the New Inn where he remained as the publican until 1869. William Poll was at the Bull longer than any of the other publicans and ran the inn for twenty eight years. He died in 1900 at the age of seventy two and was buried in St Michael's churchyard on the 29th August. His widow Adelaide, died aged 76 years in 1908.

Documentary details of the Bull prior to the 1900s has not been found, however information about the interior at the time of its closure has been discovered. The ground floor had a tap room on the left of a central passage with beer barrels at the rear and a door divided in half with a shelf for beer mugs. This room had benches and a long table where patrons played a variety of games. Opposite the tap room, a larger room had a flagstone floor, benches and tables. A room at the rear was furnished with a carpet, a sofa and comfortable chairs and on one wall, an open fireplace with a mahogany surround. The central passageway led to the kitchen from which a staircase ascended to the upper floor. Cooking for the household took place on a range and in a wall oven and a large pantry was used for domestic supplies. From the kitchen, a door opened into a yard where a wash house was situated at the end of a red tiled path. Six bedrooms were on the first floor with the largest at the stairhead, and a smaller one at the front of the building overlooked Red Lion Street. The other bedrooms led off from a passage and all the rooms had small latticed windows.

A yard behind the inn had stables, one with a hay loft, a cartshed and three toilets for the use of the publican's family and customers. Water came from a well and was heated to provide baths for the household which were taken in a tin bath in front of a bedroom fire. Beyond the yard lay a garden, principally for the use of the publican, but also available to others patronising the inn.

The Bull passed from private owners into the ownership of brewery companies and was sold after its closure. The ground floor front was converted into a fishmonger's shop and later acquired by Arthur J. Dazely as the Old Bull Motor and Cycle Works. He was replaced by George and Alan Cooper who had moved from their bicycle shop at the Feathers and they hired out and sold motor cars. After the Bull and the New Inn were demolished in 1955, the firm of Cooper developed both sites to expand their car sales business.

THE NEW INN AND KING'S HEAD

PUBLICAN		OWNER	

KING'S HEAD

Matthew Dye	1689
Richard Robertson (or Roberson)	1700
Jonathan Scottow	1773-1780
Susannah Boon (or Book)	1780-1784
William Copeman	1784-1786
Mary Copeman	1789-1790
William Strain	1790-1791

The name of the King's Head was changed to the New Inn in 1791.

THE NEW INN

William Strain	1791-1794		
John Bircham	1794		
Widow Elizabeth Strain	1796-1805		
Samuel Scotter	1830-1843		
Allen Pye	1843-1846	William Hardy	1838
Dick Feek + horsebreaker	1848-1869	W. Cozens-Hardy	1842-1895
John Watson	1872-1875	Morgan's Brewery	1896
William Jay	1879-1888		
Robert Bullock	1890-1891		
William Kemp	1892		
Mrs Kemp	1893		
Walter Barnard	1896-1900		
Mrs Eugenie Barnard	1904-1916		
William Herbert Flood	1925		
William Sheridan Selby Fairhead	1937-1953		

The New Inn closed in 1953

The New Inn, situated at 10 Red Lion Street, was known as the King's Head until William Strain advertised the change of name in the *Norwich Mercury* on the 26th November 1791. It was a fine timber framed building, dating from 1689 and possibly earlier.

Although the early layout of the interior has not been documented, information from the 1940s until its closure has been obtained. During this period, the public bar on the right of the ground floor, had a wood floor, benches against the walls and separate tables. A window faced directly on to Red Lion Street and customers could obtain beer to be consumed on a small paved area on the street, and this was served from barrels placed on trestles near to the window. A smaller room, on the left of the front passage within the building, was the saloon bar with wrought iron tables and individual chairs.

The publican's family accomodation comprised a sitting room at the front, a rear living room and a scullery with access to a yard with a wash house. The first floor had five bedrooms, but there had originally been a further three extending over an archway across Blofield's Loke. These three rooms had at sometime been converted into a flat with a living room, kitchen and bedroom, and entry was from an upper passage in the inn. Although the New Inn had accommodated guests in its early years, by the 1900s this trade had ceased and it had become known as a public house with only day and evening trade.

The area at the rear of the inn extended as far as Oakfield Road with a yard, stables, outbuildings, a garden and a bowling green. One building, the Foresters Hall, was used for club meetings and a number of social events. It is now used as a car workshop, but everything else has vanished under the present Burgh Road car park. In its time the bowling green was the venue for many matches between clubs affiliated to other inns and public houses. It was also the site of a travelling theatre, brought to Aylsham once a year for a few days after Christmas in the latter 1800s, by a Mrs Abbott. This theatre was a large waterproof canvas tent with a wooden structure and a stage that unfolded. The floor was covered in sawdust and the seats arranged in order of admission charges. The most expensive seats at the front had cushions, the middle priced had a covering of green baize and the cheapest were plain wood and made up the back rows. Heating was provided by an iron coke burning stove, and the most expensive seats were placed near to it for the enjoyment of those who paid the most. For many Aylsham residents and those from nearby villages, Mrs Abbott's theatre was their only opportunity to see a theatrical performance as, although there were theatres in Norwich, few could afford the fare or indeed the price of the tickets.

The New Inn changed over the years, but the many publicans who were responsible for the day to day running of the inn, on the whole remained for a number of years. One was Dick Feek, who was there from 1848 until 1869. In 1841, he lived in Hungate Street and was a horsedealer and horsebreaker, but by 1843 he had become the publican of the Bull Inn until he moved to the New Inn. He was obviously popular for he is mentioned in a song with words by William Mileham to commemorate the celebration of Oakapple Day on the 29th May while he was at the New Inn. Oakapple Day was observed in Aylsham as a public holiday when the various Friendly Societies paraded their banners, accompanied by the town band. All the inns and public houses decorated their frontages and bars with oak branches. Food and liquid refreshments were available to the inhabitants, bowls matches and other games were played and the evening ended with dances. Dick Feek is the only publican commemorated on Oakapple Day in this manner and he continued at the New Inn until his death in March 1869 at the age of 69 years. His wife Mary Ann had died four years before in December 1865 aged 52 years.

William Jay was the publican from 1879-1888 and in the census of 1881 gives his occupation as innkeeper. He and his wife Hannah had five children, the eldest was Arthur aged fifteen and surprisingly still at school when many of his age were either apprentices or employed in a job. There was one general domestic servant, Letitia Tudman and a lodger John Rooke, who was a harnessmaker journeyman. Another publican was Robert Bullock at the New Inn from 1890-1891 who had formerly been at the Stonemason's Arms in Millgate. In 1891 Robert Bullock was forty seven years of age and his wife Annie Frances, two years older. Living with them in the New Inn at this time were three children from Annie's first marriage to Richard Laxen (refer to the Stonemasons) and the two children, Sidney Augustus and Maggie Elizabeth from the Bullock marriage. Robert and Annie Bullock are not listed at the inn after 1891, but a Norfolk Directory lists Annie as having a fancy stationary shop in Red Lion Street in 1896. She continued in this business until the 1900s and died on the 15th March 1921 aged seventy nine.

The last publican of the New Inn was William Sheridan Selby Fairhead who was there from 1937 until it closed in 1953. For two years the building remained vacant and was then demolished along with the Bull and a car salesroom erected upon the site, so sadly two of Aylsham's old historic inns have been lost.

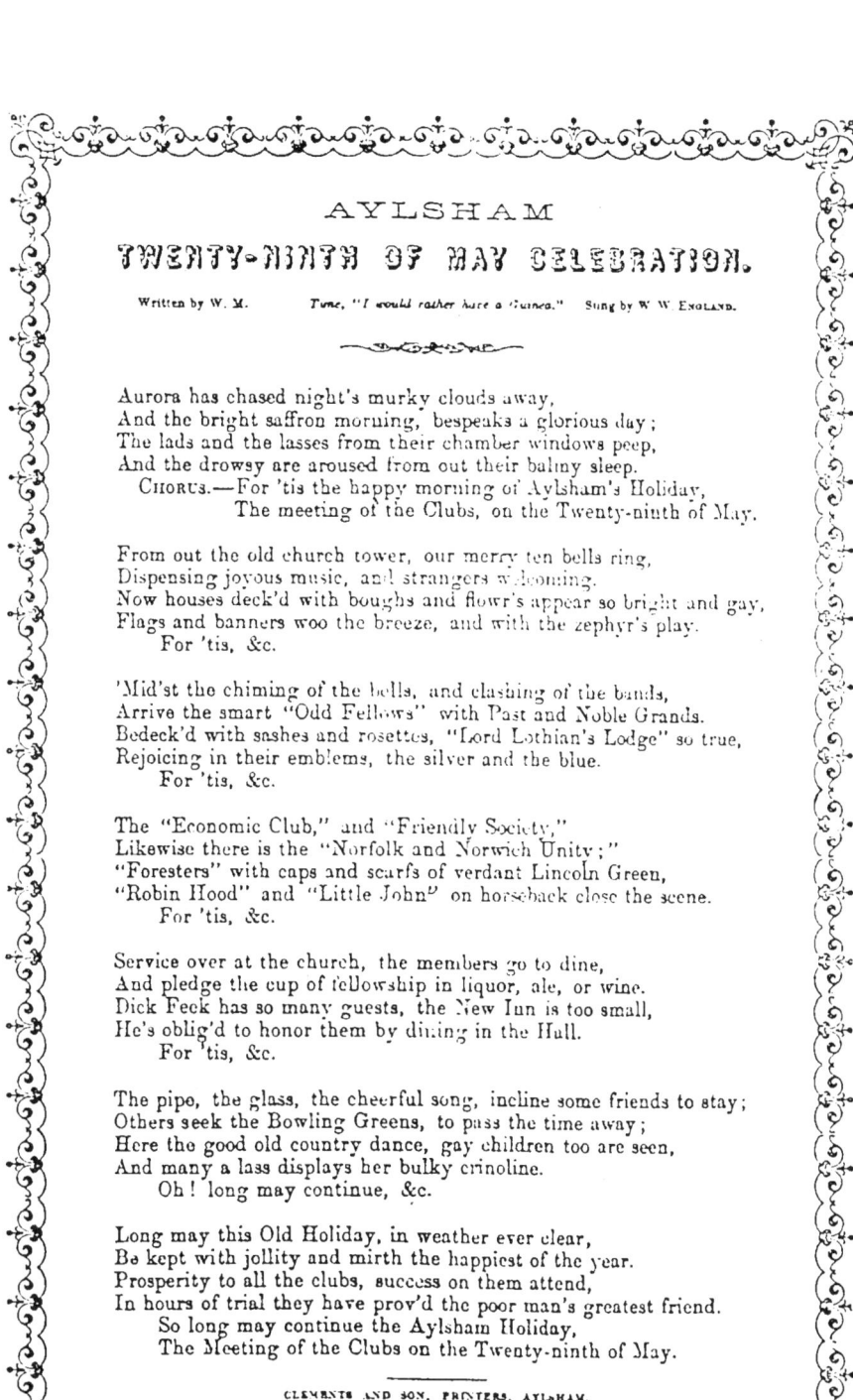

AYLSHAM
TWENTY-NINTH OF MAY CELEBRATION.

Written by W. M.   Tune, "*I would rather have a Guinea.*"   Sung by W. W. England.

Aurora has chased night's murky clouds away,
And the bright saffron morning, bespeaks a glorious day;
The lads and the lasses from their chamber windows peep,
And the drowsy are aroused from out their balmy sleep.
 Chorus.—For 'tis the happy morning of Aylsham's Holiday,
   The meeting of the Clubs, on the Twenty-ninth of May.

From out the old church tower, our merry ten bells ring,
Dispensing joyous music, and strangers welcoming.
Now houses deck'd with boughs and flowr's appear so bright and gay,
Flags and banners woo the breeze, and with the zephyr's play.
 For 'tis, &c.

'Mid'st the chiming of the bells, and clashing of the bands,
Arrive the smart "Odd Fellows" with Past and Noble Grands.
Bedeck'd with sashes and rosettes, "Lord Lothian's Lodge" so true,
Rejoicing in their emblems, the silver and the blue.
 For 'tis, &c.

The "Economic Club," and "Friendly Society,"
Likewise there is the "Norfolk and Norwich Unity;"
"Foresters" with caps and scarfs of verdant Lincoln Green,
"Robin Hood" and "Little John" on horseback close the scene.
 For 'tis, &c.

Service over at the church, the members go to dine,
And pledge the cup of fellowship in liquor, ale, or wine.
Dick Feek has so many guests, the New Inn is too small,
He's oblig'd to honor them by dining in the Hall.
 For 'tis, &c.

The pipe, the glass, the cheerful song, incline some friends to stay;
Others seek the Bowling Greens, to pass the time away;
Here the good old country dance, gay children too are seen,
And many a lass displays her bulky crinoline.
 Oh! long may continue, &c.

Long may this Old Holiday, in weather ever clear,
Be kept with jollity and mirth the happiest of the year.
Prosperity to all the clubs, success on them attend,
In hours of trial they have prov'd the poor man's greatest friend.
 So long may continue the Aylsham Holiday,
   The Meeting of the Clubs on the Twenty-ninth of May.

CLEMENTS AND SON, PRINTERS, AYLSHAM.

A poem written by W. M. Mileham to celebrate Oakapple Day at the New Inn.
(Copyright Aylsham Town Council)

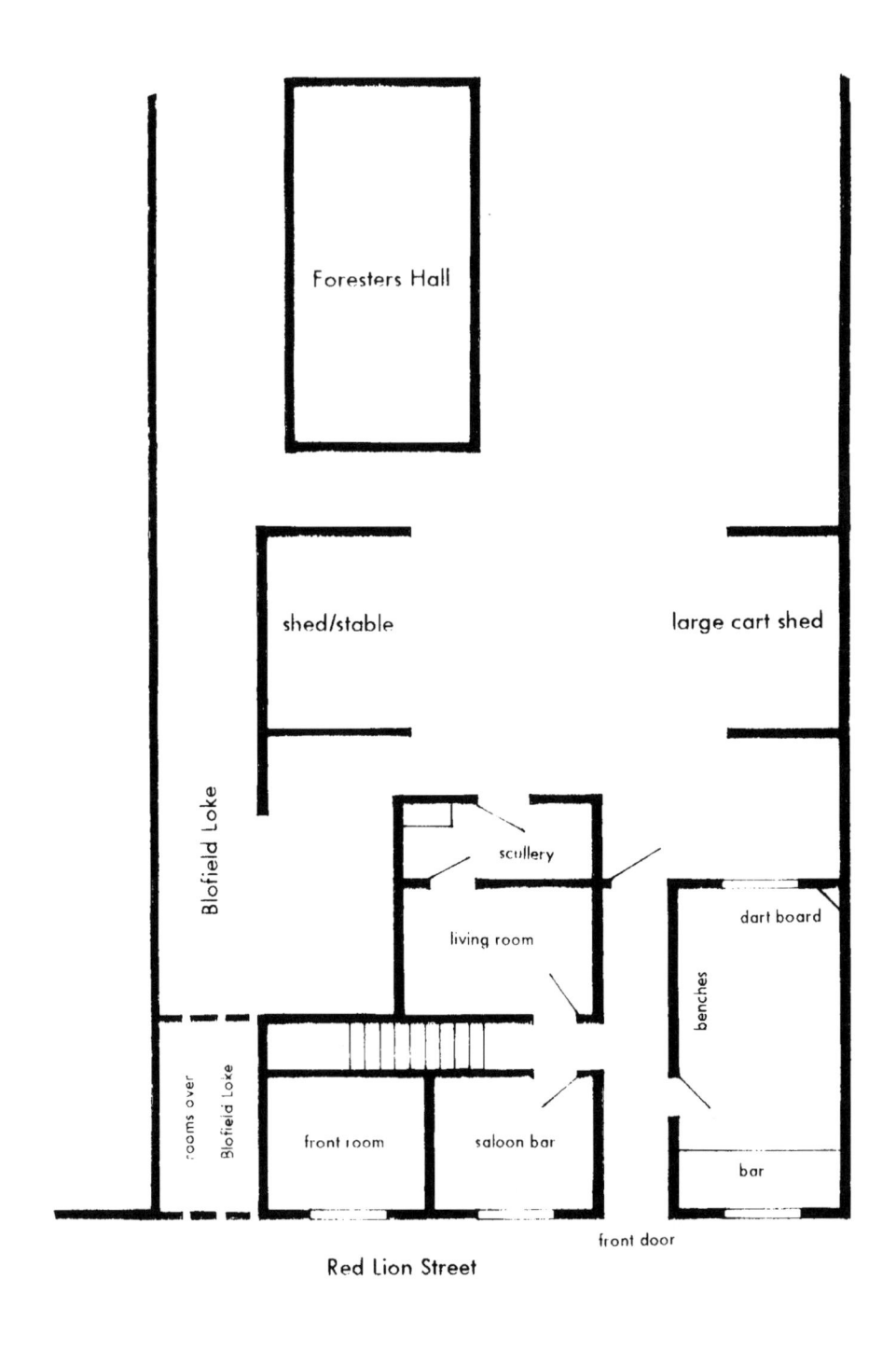

Plan of the New Inn before it closed in 1953.
(By permission of Diana Newstead)

54

THE CROSS KEYS

PUBLICAN   ### OWNER

Walter Tompson	1620		
Robert Roofe	1767-1778		
John Ulph	1785-1791		
Sarah Ulph	1791-1820		
Benjamin Ulph	1821		
Lucy Ulph	1830-1839	Steward & Patteson	1839-1896
John Hook Ulph	1840-1869		
Elizabeth Susannah Ulph	1872-1879		
William Burrell	1881-1882		
Lucy Burrell	1883		
? Tuddenham	1884-1887		
John Hannant Cook + tailor	1888-1890		
John Taylor	1891-1896		
Harry Vince	1904		
Herbert James Williamson	1908-1912		
Ernest Kirk	1916		
Ernest Drake	1925		
William Harrison	1929		

The Cross Keys closed in 1931

The Cross Keys was situated at 28 and 30 Red Lion Street. The earliest date found for this inn is 1620 when Walter Tompson was the publican. Alterations to the building were carried out in the 18th century. This former inn and public house is a two storey red brick building with attics and a steep black glazed pantile roof. Three sash windows with glazing bars were at the front on the first floor, but the one in the centre has subsequently been filled and above are two dormer attic windows. The building has corner pilasters, wood eaves and a brick string course. The first floor had five bedrooms with three attic rooms above, two at the front and a third at the rear. A Dutch gable with a chimney stack is on the northern end of the building and a two storey wing to the east has the same shaped gable.

Photographs taken in the early 1900s show that access to the Cross Keys was directly from the street through a central door, on the right were two windows with another to the left. These photographs also show the sign of the Cross Keys extending from beneath the eaves and projecting into the street. At this time a yard at the rear had stables, cartsheds, a few outbuildings, a wash house and a toilet. Access to the yard was through an entrance on the left of the building and it remains to this day.

The early history of the Cross Keys has not been documented, but later information has been obtained in regard to the ground floor rooms. These consisted of a smoke room, a separate bar room and two other rooms, one of which was used as a club room, a large kitchen and scullery. The clubroom was used on a regular basis by various societies and for social events. One entry in the *Eastern Daily Press* newspaper for December 1893 prints the following:-
'Ringers Dinner
As usual, the ringers called on the principal people in the town for 'Christmas Boxes' and this resulted in a dinner being held in the clubroom of the Cross Keys Inn last Friday, when Host and Hostess Taylor placed dinners before the ringers and chimers to the number of sixteen. Mr C. Clements presided and Mr J. M. Roberts was Vice-Chairman. They met again on Saturday night and on both occasions touched on the handbells which were given under the leadership of Mr Robert Stackwood'.

For about 100 years, the Ulph family were the publicans at the Cross Keys and this dynasty began with John Ulph in 1785. He was succeeded by his widow Sarah in 1791 and she remained until 1820 when Benjamin Ulph became the publican. After Benjamin's death, his widow (nee Hook) continued until 1839 when her son John Hook Ulph, followed on as the publican, his widow Elizabeth Susannah, succeeded until 1879. After Elizabeth Susannah died, her son-in-law William Burrell, became the publican in 1881. The census for that year shows that William Burrell was forty five years of age and his wife Lucy was thirty six and they had three children, Richard aged ten, George nine years old and Elizabeth who was seven years of age.

The Cross Keys had passed out of the Ulph family by 1884 when a Mr Tuddenham became the publican. Many members of the Ulph family are buried in St. Michael's churchyard and the headstones on their graves read:-
'Sacred to the memory of John Ulph who died 16th December 1791 aged 41 years. Sarah Ulph his wife who died 15th April 1822 aged 71 years'.
'In memory of Joseph Hopkins late of Aldeborough who died 20th May 1813 aged 33 years. Also Benjamin Hopkins who died 11th December 1811'.
'In memory of Susannah wife of Joseph Hopkins late of Aldeborough

and daughter of John and Sarah Ulph who died 3rd November 1843 aged 65 years. Beloved and Lamented'.

The Cross Keys closed in 1931, the building was sold and the ground floor converted into shops. It is still possible to see the bracket on the front facade where the Cross Keys sign was once displayed. In 1971, this former public house was listed as a Grade II building of historic interest.

Cross Keys site in Red Lion Street.

Cross Keys 1900s.

THE STAR INN

PUBLICAN		OWNER	
Philip Penn Wilson	1829-1836		
George Clarke	1839-1854	William Primrose	1839
Robert Wortley	1854		
Richard Matthews	1856		
William Tuddenham	1863-1865	J.B. Morgan	1863-1893
Richard Riches	1868		
John Goodwin + farmer	1875-1883		
Henry John Tuddenham	1888		
Henry Jordan + carter	1890-1891		
? Doughty	1893		
William Flanders	1896		
George Grimson	1900	Morgan & Co.	1900

The Star Inn closed in 1900

The earliest documented date for this inn is 1829. It was situated at 36 Red Lion Street and was a small establishment on two floors with an entrance directly from the street. To the right, a wide entrance between the inn and the building next to it, gave access to a yard and stables at the rear. The Star premises extended from Red Lion Street in an easterly direction towards garden areas owned in 1839 by James Diggins.

Unfortunately very little has been discovered about this inn, but an entry in a Workhouse Book in the Aylsham Archives is of interest. It records that pauper Curtis Parr, aged 21 years, was discharged on the 10th April 1829 to service at the Star Inn. In 1868 Samuel Ducker, an orphan, who later became a wheelwright and builder in White Hart Street, lived with his uncle Richard Riches at the inn.

The 1881 Census for Aylsham gives information about the occupants of the Star at that time. It notes that the publican John Goodwin, was forty years old and also listed as a farmer, but where he farmed has not been documented. His wife Rosanna was four years younger and they had two daughters, Keziah aged eight years and Violet who was one year old. Living with them was Sarah A. Bullen, a fourteen year old domestic servant and a lodger named Peter Pike, aged thirty two years, whose occupation is given as a groom and domestic servant.

The Star Inn closed in 1900 and the premises were taken over by Pask and Sons, a tailoring business which catered exclusively for the needs of the more affluent residents of Aylsham, and those from surrounding villages; it continued in business until at least 1937. This former inn, has been divided into three commercial enterprises, one is a shop with direct entry from Red Lion Street and was the main entrance to the inn and the other two are situated at the rear of the building. The entrance, where horses were led through to be stabled in the rear yard, has been retained and adjoins the buildings on each side.

Site of the Star Inn 1995

THE RED LION

PUBLICAN		OWNER	
John Allen	1700		
William Rannells	1723		
Thomas Dix	1730-1737		
Widow Alice Dix	1762		
Watts Austin	1771-1805		
James Butler	1830		
William Legood	1836-1839	Robert Hawes	1839
Hannah Legood	1839		
John Chapman + butcher	1843-1853		
George Clark	1853-1863		
Robert Osborne	1864	John Chapman	1864
John Cooper	1864-1869		
Christmas Stapleton	1872-1877	William Primrose	1872
Miles Augustus Baker + Veterinary Surgeon MRCVS	1877-1882	Primrose Executors	1877-1900
Edward Woodhouse	1883-1900		
Frederick William Sole	1900		
Miles Hall	1908-1921		
Richard R. Bone	1925		
Captain Richard Beard	1930-1936	Trunch Brewery	1930-1950
Thomas Edward Slipper	1937		
Albert Murton	1937-1958	Morgan & Co.	1952
Joe Smith	1961-1972		

The Red Lion closed in 1972

The earliest date known for the Red Lion at 31 Red Lion Street is 1700. After it closed in 1972, the premises were converted into shops with a flat above and it is now a Grade II listed building. The roof line indicates that the original Red Lion was much smaller and that at a later date, the building on the right was incorporated to extend the premises. These two steeped pantile roofs are at different levels, and the line of bricks are not continuous indicating two separate buildings. Built of red brick the facades are now colourwashed. No early evidence regarding the appearance of the building has been found, but photographs taken in the early 1900s give some indication of what it was like. The ground floor had two front entrances which gave direct access from the street and between these there were two small paned windows. A larger window was on the right of the second door, while the upper floor had a big window on the left and two smaller ones on the right hand side.

Although the Red Lion is listed in early documents as an inn, by the late 1800s it was known as an hotel. At this time a wrought iron bracket extended outwards from the building and carried a sign for

the Red Lion Hotel and the name of William Primrose who was the owner. This hotel was a smaller establishment than either the Black Boys or the Dog where accomodation was also offered. In 1868, the publican John Cooper advertised:-
'Red Lion - Family and Commercial Hotel and Posting House. Wines and spirits of the best quality. Well aired beds and moderate charges'.

By 1930 the Trunch Brewery owned the Red Lion and the Primrose sign had been removed and replaced with one affixed to the front wall. In addition a narrow board above the windows on the ground floor advertised the Trunch Brewery bottled ales and stouts. The Red Lion had by this time ceased to be either an inn or hotel and was classified as a public house. The interior prior to 1930 has not been recorded, but details from this period are known. There were three rooms at the front overlooking Red Lion Street, one a public bar or tap room had two long tables and wooden benches on a wood floor. Beer barrels were placed on trestles at the rear of this bar and all customers were served their drinks from a shelved half door. The second room was the lounge bar, furnished with individual tables and chairs. Both rooms were warmed by log or coal fires, and the third room was for the private use of the publican. Another three rooms including a kitchen overlooked the rear yard with an underground cellar extending below the building. The first floor had six bedrooms, a bathroom and two attic rooms. The lighting of all the rooms in the early days of the Red Lion was by candles, then gas and finally by electricity.

Access to the rear yard was from Red Lion Street through a wide entrance on the left of the building. In this yard there were stables and cartsheds, where farmers from outlying areas left their horses and carts or ponies and traps in the care of the publican while they attended Aylsham market. There were other buildings in the yard including a wash house and a men's toilet. A well in the centre of the yard supplied water for the household and for the horses, but fell into disuse when a mains water supply was installed in 1938, the well has since been filled in.

A separate building in the Red Lion yard was known as a function room. This building was on two floors with the ground floor used for storage and a toilet; stairs led to a large room on the upper floor where various club meetings and social events took place. One club that held monthly meetings in the function room of the Red Lion was the Aylsham and Buxton Rowing Club which was formed on the 9th June 1871 with Dr. R. K. Morton as the Commodore. During the summer months, regattas were held on the River Bure, but the club was wound up in 1876 after trouble with six young men who were members. It would appear that they were a persistent source of trouble and embarrassment to the other members as they damaged a boat belonging to the club, broke oars, lost rowlocks and left the boat in a filthy condition.

An extract from the *Eastern Daily Press* newspaper for the 2nd January 1893 gives the following information:-

'FIREMEN'S DINNER - The members of the Aylsham Brigade had their annual dinner at the clubroom of the Red Lion Inn, provided by Host and Hostess Woodhouse. Mr. Arthur Neale presided and a pleasant evening was spent. The expense was defrayed from subscriptions collected on Boxing Day and the firemen wish to thank all those who contributed'.

From the *Aylsham and District Almanack* 1904.
'A. J. March, Red Lion Hotel Yard, Aylsham.
Residence: Town Lane. Job Master and Carrier to Norwich.
Mondays, Wednesdays and Saturdays (Friday on special occasions) Horses and Traps, Cabs and Waggonettes for hire for large or small parties. Household Furniture and General Goods removed on reasonable terms. Orders received by Post or Telegram immediately attended to'.

From the *Aylsham and District Illustrated Almanack and Companion* 1906.
'April - The members of the Aylsham Town Football Club having been successful in winning the shield and medals of the Northern Junior Division, celebrated their victory with a dinner at the Red Lion Hotel under the presidency of Mr W. W. S. Follet. After the meal, the shield was presented by Mr Rippingall to Captain Pegg on behalf of the club and medals were afterwards handed to the following members:- Messrs. Dove, Ford, Pumphrey, Partridge, Cornall, Goulden, Williment, Seely, Rackham, Pegg, Humphreys and Pask'.

'May - 3rd VB Norfolk Regiment (C. Company) Captain Thomas Woods Purdy, Commanding. Sergeant-Major W. Monument, Drill Instructor.

The Red Lion after its closure in 1972.
(By permission of the Aylsham Association)

Following the weekly drill of the Company on the 9th May, the members were invited by Captain Purdy to supper at the Red Lion Hotel clubroom'.

In 1923, the Aylsham Ex-Service Men's Club affiliated to the British Legion held its meetings in the Red Lion function room during the hours of 6 p.m. to 10.30 p.m. on all weekdays. On Wednesdays and Saturdays, the hours were from 2 p.m. to 10.30 p.m. It is not clear how other meetings fitted in with those of the Ex-Servicemen's Club. After the Aylsham Town Band was formed, the function room was used for a regular weekly practice. When the Red Lion closed another venue was found for the band to continue practising. Other clubs also had to find new locations in which to continue their meetings.

Some details of a few Red Lion publicans have emerged and one is Watts Austin, a butcher who was the publican from 1771-1805. In 1770, he had been granted a 14 year lease at £1 4s 0d per annum by William Spurrell, a baker of Norwich, of a pightle and 1 acre of land next to the Buttlands lately occupied by William Clarke, also a baker. The lease included the protection of timber on the land. Another publican at the Red Lion from 1877-1882 was Miles Augustus Baker, a veterinary surgeon.

He was born in Holt in 1852 and his wife Harriet had been born in Buxton in 1851. The 1881 census of Aylsham shows that Miles Baker had a stepson, Hiram Watson aged eight years and two children, Miles C. Baker who was two years old and a daughter Susie of only a few months of age. Sharing the Baker household were two general domestic servants, Emma Hall who was nineteen and fifteen year old Kesiah King.

Many changes came about in subsequent years and by 1930, the Red Lion had ceased to operate as an hotel. In this year, Captain Richard Beard, who had formerly been the publican at the Black Boys, came to the Red Lion which was owned at that time by the Trunch Brewery. During the day Captain Beard travelled around Norfolk in a Trojan car obtaining orders for the brewery company and in the evenings served behind the bar of the Red Lion. His wife Violet was responsible for the day to day running of the public house, provided refreshments for lunch time customers, catered for social events, club dinners and some wedding receptions. After six years, Captain and Mrs Beard left the Red Lion, moved to a bungalow which he had built in the Blickling Road and he went to work for the National Trust. Richard Beard devoted his spare time to music and played in the orchestra of the Cromer and Sheringham Operatic and Dramatic Society, and also had his own dance band. In his retirement he became proficient at repairing and making violins. He also wrote articles under the pseudonym of 'Master Mariner' for the *Eastern Daily Press* newspaper, and many of his stories about his time as an officer in the Mercantile Service were broadcast on the BBC. For his service in two world wars, he was awarded the MBE by King George VI in 1946. Papers and documents relating to the life of Captain Beard are in the Aylsham Town Archives.

Albert Murton, a retired police officer and ex-cavalry man was the Red Lion publican from 1937-1958 and it was well known that he kept a sabre behind the bar in case of trouble. During World War II, blackout curtains covered the doors and windows and the front entrances were kept locked so that customers had to come into the Red Lion through a back door. Many soldiers and airmen stationed around Aylsham visited in their off duty hours and some joined in games of darts with the regular customers. There was a keen darts team who played in competitions with other public house teams and when the Red Lion closed they transferred to the Stonemasons in Millgate.

The site of the former Red Lion 1995.

THE SHIP

PUBLICAN		OWNER	
James Webster	1792-1795	Maria Allen	1864-1873
? Tuttington	1796	M.A. Allen heirs	1891-1893
Joseph Bird	1856-1867	Morgan Brewery Co. Ltd.	1900-1960
Elizabeth Bird	1868-1883	Bullard & Sons Ltd.	1961
George Bird	1888-1892	Watney Mann (East Anglia) Ltd.	1967
Widow G. Bird	1893	Norwich Brewery Ltd.	1976
Rebecca Bird	1896-1900	Norwich Brewery Co. Ltd.	1982-1987
W. Curtis	1900		
Henry Brown	1904		
Sophia Turner	1908		
Frederick Bland	1912		
Herbert James Williamson	1916		
Edward Clarence Buck	1925-1933		
Albert V. Traher	1933-1937		
Len Howard	1950-1960		
Annie Howard	1960-1980		
Captain Brown	1980-1983		

The Ship closed in 1983

The earliest date found for the Ship is 1792 and it was known as an inn, but classified later as an hotel. This inn was at 13 White Hart Street and re-built in 1902 in the Edwardian style of architecture. As an hotel in the early 1900s, it offered comfortable bedrooms, breakfast, lunch, tea and dinner. There were four bedrooms and a bathroom for guests on the first floor and a 28ft. x 14ft. function room. The ground floor had two bars, the Smoke Room and Snug, a kitchen and private rooms for the publican. Entrance to the Smoke Room was directly from White Hart Street and the Snug was entered by a door on the corner of the building. The doors to these two bars have been retained and are of Edwardian design with the bottom sections of wood and the upper part of each door has narrow panes of mottled glass. At the top and bottom, the corners have inlets of coloured glass and the centre glass panels of the individual doors are etched with the words Smoke Room and Snug.

The building is built of red brick with decorative features in the brickwork, a pantile roof and underneath the eaves on the front facade are timber beams and a small centre gable. There are four windows on the ground floor and the same number above on the first floor, where from between two of them, a sign hung facing into White Hart Street. The beams at the front are echoed at the side of the building where there were two windows on the first floor and on the ground floor a window and a door, which has subsequently been filled in. A wide entrance on the left of the Ship gave access to the rear yard, where once beer barrels were delivered to an underground cellar, and there were stables, cartsheds and outbuildings, but this area has been developed in recent years with housing.

The function room was used for meetings, social events and wedding receptions. The *Aylsham and District Illustrated Almanack and Companion* for 1904 gives the details of one event:
'3rd VB Norfolk Regiment (C Company) Hon. Major Henry James Gidney, Commanding, Thomas Woods Purdy, Lieutenant, Sergeant Major W. Monument, Drill Instructor.
Following the weekly drill of the Company on the 10th May, the Major invited the men to spend the remainder of the evening with him at the 'Ship Hotel'. Refreshments and tobacco were provided, and a pleasant time was spent in toast and song. Regret was expressed at the inability of ex-Sergeant Major Brawn to meet his old comrades, owing to a serious illness'.

By 1968, the Ship Hotel was only offering bed and breakfast accomodation to guests, but Mrs Annie Howard the publican, also provided lunches and these were particularly popular with commercial travellers who came to Aylsham on business. The function room continued to be used as in the past, but eventually this part of the business was phased out, and it operated as a public house until it closed in 1983. After the closure, the Norwich Brewery Co. Ltd. who owned the building, leased the ground floor to John and Patricia Postle as workshop premises for their radio, TV and electrical goods business. The Norwich Brewery Co. Ltd. sold the building to Andrew and Jill Kemp in 1987 and they continued to lease the ground floor to J. B. Postle until 1992 when for a time it became a centre for those suffering from mental illness.

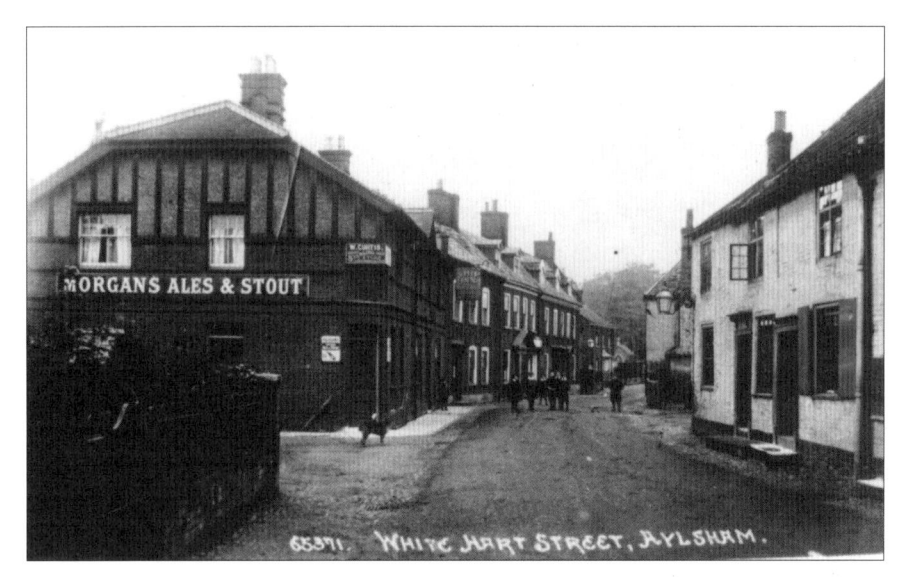

The Ship in 1902

The Ship 1970.
(By permission of the Aylsham Association)

THE WHITE HART INN

PUBLICAN		OWNER	
John Bishop	1691	Jonathan Ulph	1737-1740
Philip Hart	1693	William Bircham	1839
Nicholas Bullard	1700		
James Fish	1730		
Jonathan Ulph	1737-1740		
Benjamin Bush	1745		
Stephen Bush	1749-1750		
Mary Bush	1752-1781		
Robert Dodman	1781-1821		
William Pratt	1839		
Everett Pearson	1843-1846		
Robert Jarvies + clothier	1850		
William Brown	1853		

The White Hart closed between 1853-1864

The White Hart Inn was situated at 19 White Hart Street, formerly known as Chapel Street, close to Town Lane and the earliest date found for it is 1691. Although the publicans can be named from the late 1600s, the owners remain relatively unknown and it may be that some of the publicans also owned the property. A description of the White Hart as it was in 1740 can be ascertained from the will of Jonathan Ulph, who was at the inn from 1737-1740. His will dated 26th March 1740 is as follows:-
'Will of Jonathan Ulph, millwright of Aylsham.
Bequethed soul to God hoping for salvation through the merits of Jesus Christ.
To brother Joseph 1 shilling
To wife Mary and daughter Mary all my land in Aylsham and all my goods and chattels.
To my mother Mary Bowers, the dwelling in my workshop in Aylsham for life.
Executries: Mother and wife.'

A probate inventory made a month later gives the following:-
'Probate inventory of Jonathan Ulph, millwright of Aylsham made 8th April 1740.
Appraisors: Thomas Hawkins and Jonathan Custons.
Total value: £166.13s.6d
Rooms: kitchen, parlour, shop, buttery, great parlour, pantry, cellar, dairy.
In the White Hart brewhouse, brewing vessels, (including a copper)

barrels, hogsheads etc.
Stable, barn (15 combs barley) 5 acres of corn on the ground.'

One publican of the White Hart was Robert Dodman who came to Aylsham in 1779 with his wife Elizabeth and one year old daughter named Virtue. They had a settlement certificate from their parish of Foulsham, which meant that if they became paupers, Aylsham would not be responsible for their financial support. By 1781 Robert Dodman had become the publican of the White Hart. Virtue grew up in Aylsham and married John Boyers, the spelling of this surname was later changed to Bowers. In 1804 John Bowers was transported for life to one of the British colonies for committing a felony and left his young wife in Aylsham. Six years later, with her husband serving his life sentence, Virtue became pregnant and gave birth to a son whom she named Robert.

A bastardy bond dated 2nd June 1811 was signed jointly by Thomas Soame, a member of the wealthy Soame family of Aylsham and Robert Dodman, Virtue's father. This bond guaranteed financial support from Thomas Soame, undoubtedly the father of Virtue's child, so that she was not reliant on parish charity. The law of 1733, stipulated that a woman, unmarried, widowed or with an absent husband, must name the father of her child. This law compelled the father to pay maintenance for his child and failure to do so would result in a term of imprisonment. Virtue's son retained her surname of Bowers and became a carpenter, wheelwright, carver and gilder. He married Matilda, a straw bonnet maker and they lived at premises on Church Hill, as it was then named. Church Hill was located at the junction of what is now the Cromer Road, Red Lion Street and White Hart Street.

Robert Dodman was a religious man and an entry recorded in the Aylsham Dissenters Register for 1796 gives the following information:-
'On the 18th July 1796, it was certified by Robert Dodman, wheelwright, that a certain building formerly used as a hay barn and called a hay house and now in part newly erected and now enlarged standing in the yard belonging to his now dwelling house situate in the street called the White Hart Street and is by him designated and set apart as a place of religious worship for protestant dissenters'.

On the 20th March 1830, Elizabeth, the wife of Robert Dodman died at the age of seventy and a year later he died on the 10th April aged eighty; they are both buried in St. Michael's churchyard. Virtue Bowers and her son continued living in Aylsham and the James Wright map of 1839 shows that at this time they both owned a considerable amount of property. The properties owned by Virtue were houses in Town Lane, one with a garden which she occupied and the other houses, a shop, shed and gardens were rented by tenants. Robert Bowers owned and occupied a house and shop at the corner of Church Hill near to the lychgate of St Michael's church. In addition he had a further four houses and a yard in this same area which he leased or let to tenants. It has not been possible to establish how Virtue and Robert Bowers acquired so much property. The Norfolk Directories list them in Aylsham until 1850, but they are not mentioned in later editions.

Unfortunately, no documentary evidence of what the White Hart was like has been discovered. It was certainly used in later times as a venue for farmers coming to Aylsham from their farms near the northern end of the town. There were stables, cartsheds and outbuildings at the rear with an entrance to these in Town Lane, where horses and carts could be accommodated while the farmers attended to their business in the town. All that is known is that in the 1800s, the White Hart was a two storey building built of red brick with a pantile roof, chimney stack, sash windows and had attic dormer windows above. Access to the inn was through a front door directly from the street.

By 1864, the White Hart had closed and the premises were converted into a pork butcher's shop with a large window inserted at the front of the building. The butcher was William Barber who was succeeded in 1875 by William Flint. He was followed by Robert Goodwin 1879-1904, Sidney Bailey in 1912 and George Briggs 1916-1933. Today the former White Hart Inn and butcher's shop have been converted into a private residence, and changes to the brickwork show the infill after the removal of the shop window. The area behind the building where there were once stables and cartsheds has been built upon in recent years.

The former White Hart site 1970.
(By permission of the Aylsham Association)

THE BREWERY

PUBLICAN		OWNER	
Mary King + brewer	1830		
Henry Poll + brewer	1839-1868	Henry Poll	1839-1868
Robert Nicholls + brewer	1868	James B. Chappell	1868-1890
William Cooper, brewer + maltster	1872-1879	James B. Chappell Exc.	1891-1901
Samuel Ducker	1879-1904	Youngs Crawshay & Youngs	1901-1907

The Brewery closed in 1907

The Brewery public house which closed in 1907 was at 23 White Hart Street and, although the details of the interior are unknown, it probably had one or two small bar rooms. The building is built of red brick with a grey pantile roof with a chimney stack at each end, and on the front facade two sash windows on the ground floor situated on each side of the door. This door has a porch constructed of wood and glass and dates from the Victorian or Edwardian era. The first floor has three sash windows directly above the lower windows and the door. To the left, fronting on to White Hart Street, is the former brewhouse dating to the late 1700s. This long red brick building has flint infills on the outer west wall, a number of windows on two floors and a bricked up doorway. The building lies parallel to Town Lane and beyond are two other buildings, once the stables and cart shed. Between this former brewhouse and the Brewery building is an opening which allows access to a rear yard.

In 1836, Henry Poll a brewer, owned the whole site and also rented another brewhouse and outbuildings owned by Edward Jarvis in 1839, these premises were in an area behind the Ship in White Hart Street. In addition that same year, he rented from William Blyth, a house, stable and cartshed situated opposite the Ship, these have since been demolished. Henry Poll was also a tenant of a garden owned by Deborah Soame at the bottom of Town Lane and a house now stands on this site.

James B. Chappell bought the Brewery property from Henry Poll in 1868 and William Cooper, a brewer and maltster was the occupier until 1879. In that year Samuel Ducker, a carpenter and wheelwright, took over the tenancy. He was not a brewer and used the brewhouse for his wheelwright, carpentry and light cart making business. By 1891, James B. Chappell had died and his executors retained the premises until 1901 when the brewery company of Youngs, Crawshay

& Youngs bought all the buildings. Samuel Ducker remained a tenant, but by 1904 had moved to Millgate where he carried on his business.

The Brewery public house closed in 1907 and Youngs, Crawshay & Youngs offered the premises for sale. Samuel Ducker purchased the property and moved back again to 23 White Hart Street. In addition to his carpentry and wheelwright business, Samuel Ducker developed the building side of the firm. He was joined in partnership with his son Stanley Samuel in about 1927. When Samuel Ducker died in 1936, his son carried on the business and on his death in 1948, he was succeeded by his son Geoffrey. Ducker's Funeral Services had been established on the old Brewery public house site. On his retirement, Geoffrey Ducker sold the property to Gray and Cooper who continued the funeral services and retained the name of Ducker.

The former Brewery, White Hart Street.

AYLSHAM, *Xmas* 1891.

W. Forster Esq.

Dr. to SAMUEL DUCKER,
CARPENTER, WHEELWRIGHT, LIGHT CART MAKER,
AND GENERAL BUILDER.

WHEELS MADE TO ORDER, OF THE BEST MATERIALS.

Feb 11	Saw sharping		4
20	Wheel Barrow Rep & Shafts splicing	2	6
	New water tub for Greenhouse	3	6
Mar 20	6 New oak Posts 6½ ft long squared to 4½ in	18	0
	7 new spurs	3	6
	14 ft 3 in Deal 9 wide for Rails	8	0
	15 ft 2½ Do 7 wide for Pales	3	9
	9 ft inch Board 11 wide	1	10
	16 ft Do 7 wide	1	8
	18 ft ¾ in Do 11 wide	3	0
	57 ft inch Do 7 wide	6	0
	36 ft 1½ in Do 7 wide for	4	6
	Rep Railing Boarding & new Door by		
	8 ft Deal 3 in 9 wide	4	0
	4 ft 2 in oak 6 in wide	1	6
	24 ft inch Board 7 wide	2	6
	for frame & Door to Stoke hole		
	10 lbs nails	2	6
	2 Days labour to same	1 8	0
	New oak threshold 4 ft long 3 in 5 in wide	2	6
	15 new oak Posts 5 ft long		
		1 10	0

Part of a bill from Samuel Ducker to W. Parmenter 1891.

THE WHITE HORSE

PUBLICAN		OWNER	
William Kilby	1620		
Thomas Hallifore	1670-1700		
Thomas Forster	1723-1734	Thomas Forster	1723-1734
Charles Forster	1723-1734		
Mary Forster	1734-1736		
Mary Spinks	1740		
William Rannalls	1741-1742		
Widow Rannalls	1743-1761		
James Curties	1762-1771		
William Wiseman	1771-1772		
Mary Bush	1773-1781		
Clement Ives	1781-1785		
Edward Phillips	1785-1786		
James Curties	1786		
Frederick Gedge	1787-1788		
John Eager	1788-1791	William Bircham	1840
Robert Hagon	1843-1846		
William Cook Stangroom	1850		
John Nicholls, butcher + farmer	1850-1888	Bircham & Son	1872-1874
Susannah Nicholls + butcher	1890-1900	Steward & Patteson	1882-1906
Stanley Nicholls + butcher	1904-1906		

The White Horse closed in 1906

The White Horse was situated at numbers 1 and 1a Millgate. Although dating from the 1600s, it was probably re-built in the 1800s and classified as a beerhouse, but later re-named as a public house. It was a small detached building on two floors, a narrow two storey extension was added at a later date. The front facade of red brick and small sea coastal stones had a central front door, a single window on the left and a double sized window to the right. Two single windows on the first floor were situated directly above those on the ground floor. A small forecourt adjacent to the road led to the front door, and a wide entrance on the left gave access to the rear yard.

Unfortunately there is no documentary evidence of the interior, but as it was a small establishment, it is likely to have had only one bar room which would have been furnished with benches, a long central table or small separate tables placed on a flagstone floor. In 1850, a sign outside depicted a white horse, but this had disappeared by the 1900s and been replaced by a long narrow board above the right hand window on the ground floor.

It has been possible to obtain information about some of the White Horse publicans from the Aylsham Archives. William Rannells, the publican from 1741-1742, came from the Red Lion in Red Lion Street and is listed as owning a malthouse in Aylsham from 1725-1730. He was a churchwarden at St Michael's church from 1742 until his death in 1743. His widow succeeded him at the White Horse and remained the publican for the next eighteen years. In 1850, John Nicholls became the publican and he was also a butcher. The property at that time, not only included the public house, but on land behind there were stables, cartsheds, a wash house, slaughterhouse, sheep pens, outbuildings and a yard. John Nicholls died in 1888 and was buried in St Michael's churchyard where a headstone was erected in his memory. His widow Susannah took on the role of publican and butcher and remained there until her death in 1901. She was buried beside her husband on the 23rd December. Their son Stanley carried on the tradition of publican and butcher until the White Horse was closed down by the Licensing Magistrates in 1906.

William Bircham, a Reepham brewer, had acquired the White Horse in 1840, but by 1882, the brewery company of Steward and Patteson were the owners. In 1906, they sold all the property to Arthur Edward Partridge, a butcher of Aylsham. He converted part of the former public house into a butcher's shop by removing the right hand ground floor window and installing a large shop window. This shop continued until 1958, when it was sold and the building converted into two separate cottages. The discerning eye can still detect the former shop window on the front facade of 1a Millgate as the coastal stones, which have been inserted around the present window do not match the craftsmanship of the original building. What was once the forecourt of the White Horse has been converted into two separate gardens and all traces of this former public house have now disappeared.

1 and 1a Millgate, formerly the White Horse.

THE STONEMASONS

PUBLICAN		OWNER	
John Freeman,			
stonemason + brewer	1846-1865	John Freeman	1846-1865
James Ling	1867-1872	Fanny Chapman	1865
Mrs James Ling	1873-1874		
Richard Laxen	1875-1878		
Annie Frances Laxen	1878-1879		
Robert Bullock,			
harness maker + saddler	1879-1890	Richard Chapman	1890-1926
Walter Dixon	1890-1891		
William Herbert Hammond	1892-1893		
Ernest Alfred Eastoe + clog maker	1896		
Henry Lancum	1900		
Walter Robert Neave	1904		
John U. Tinkler	1908		
George Oliver	1911-1916		
Arthur Kerry	1925		
William George Austin	1929		
Ernest William Docking	1933-1958	Steward & Patteson	1958
Donald Dyball	1958-1971	Bullards	1970
John (Jock) Cairncross	1975-1995	Norwich Brewery	1975
Pauline Hagon	1995	Brent Walker	1976-1995
		Pubmaster	1995

The Stonemasons is still operating as a public house

Information about the site on which the Stonemasons public house was built dates back to 1789 when Mary Berry, the widow of John Berry, inherited her parents property and land in Millgate. This is described as two roods of land on which was one tenement and later two tenements or cottages with an adjoining pightle. Mary Berry died in 1820 and left all her properties to the artist Joseph Clover. In about 1840, Joseph Clover sold these properties to John Freeman, a stonemason, who built a public house on the pightle of land in 1846 naming it the Stonemason's Arms. Next to the public house, he had a yard with outbuildings, further yards and a garden. In addition to being responsible for the public house and his stonemason's business, he also brewed beer. His stonemason's business was successful and in 1851, he employed men and apprentices, eight in total. John Freeman's wife Jemima, not only assisted in the running of the public house, but was also responsible for writing the bills to the clients of her husband's stonemason's business. She died in 1866 at the age of 60 years and was buried in the Aylsham Cemetery.

On the death of John Freeman, his two daughters inherited his properties. One daughter Fanny, later married Richard Chapman

Bill from John Freeman 1854

and they let the Stonemason's Arms to Messrs. Bullard & Co. Fanny Chapman died before her husband and he inherited from her the public house, the stonemason's yard, one shop and three cottages. After the death of Richard Chapman in 1926, the three cottages were bought individually by Messrs. Pert, Dyball and Atkins, but it is not known who bought the public house and the other properties.

An undated and handwritten paper found in the attic of the Stonemasons is as follows:-
'Stonemason's Arms Estate, Aylsham.
Consisting of a Public House with stabling, coach house, small piggery and garden.
Stonemason's yard with work shop. Rent £12.
Small general shop and yard and garden. Rent £13.
Three cottages total rents. £16.
The whole occupying an area of about three quarters of an acre and with a frontage about £175.
The public house is in fair condition and much better built than other portions of the property.
The shop and cottages are getting dilapidated, needing considerable repairs.
The value of the whole estate as freehold in the open market excluding the value of the license will be about £850'.

The exterior of the public house has not changed since it was built by John Freeman, and is constructed of red brick, finished with stone corners, a slate roof and a chimney stack at each end. On the ground floor at the front, there is a central door with a large window on each side with three smaller windows on the first floor placed directly above the door and the windows of the lower floor. A sign, hanging on a free standing pole on the front forecourt depicts two stonemasons at work. Various designs for this sign have been used in the past with the name 'Stonemason's Arms' boldly displayed, but now it is only known as the Stonemasons although many local people refer to it as the Stonecutters or simply the Cutters. An area to the right was once a yard where gravestones and memorial tablets were displayed, but it is now a car park. Access to the rear of the public house is through a wide entrance on the left where there were once stables, cartsheds, outbuildings and a brewhouse. In subsequent years the use of these buildings changed, one was used for a time as a fish and chip shop, another converted into toilets and the others for storage space. It is through this entrance that the beer barrels are delivered to the cellar entrance at the back of the building.

The original interior of the Stonemason's Arms had two rooms on the ground floor for the use of customers and behind the bar on the left hand side there was a small room called the Snug. Changes were made in the 1950s by the owners and a programme of modernisation was carried out. The two ground floor bar rooms were converted into one and the dividing wall to the snug was removed. In this refurbishment, the original mahogany bar counter was taken out and replaced with one considered to be more contemporary in style. In addition, the carved wood mantelpiece surrounding the open fireplace in one bar was also removed and replaced with a smaller plain one with a tiled inset. It is thought that the counter and mantelpiece, both dating to 1846, were destroyed by burning them in the rear yard and certainly no trace of them has been found. The open fireplace was however left in position and coal or log fires are still used to warm the room. Apart from this ground floor bar, there is also a kitchen and living room. The first floor has three bedrooms, a bathroom and toilet, and another room is used by the present publican as a sitting room. Stairs lead from a landing on this floor to two attic rooms and two box rooms.

There have been a few owners since John Freeman, and even more

Annie Frances Laxen/Bullock
(By permission of Derrick Baker)

publicans who were employed over the years to run the Stonemasons. Many of the latter are only names in directories, rate books and a few documents. James Ling, the publican from 1867-1872, died aged 65 years in 1873. His widow continued as the publican for a year, but died in October 1874 at the age of 62 years and was succeeded by Richard Laxen who was the publican from 1875-1878. He was born in Aylsham in 1842 into a family of saddle and harnessmakers who had a prosperous business in the Market Place. As a young man, Richard went to London as a harness maker journeyman.

While in London, Richard Laxen met Annie Frances Fenn who had been born in Southwark, London and they married on the 2nd July 1862 when they were both twenty years of age. On the marriage certificate, Richard's father is given as Henry Laxen, saddler and Annie's father as William Fenn, shoemaker. After their marriage, Annie and Richard lived in Marylebone, London and had two children, Edith in 1866 and Edwin in 1868. By 1870, Richard had returned to Aylsham with his wife and two children and had a further seven children all born in Aylsham and these were Albert R. 1870, Charles H. 1872, Ada Katie 1873, Henry Fenn 1875, Frederick W. 1877, Daisy 1878 and Robert Stanley in 1879.

In 1875, Richard Laxen became the publican of the Stonemason's Arms, but on the 24th September 1878 he died from tuberculosis at the early age of thirty seven. At the time of her husband's death, Annie was pregnant with their youngest son and remained at the Stonemasons with her children and became the publican. Fourteen months later on the 23rd November, she married Robert Bullock, a thirty five year old widower who was also a harnessmaker and he assumed the role of publican. The first child of this marriage was Sidney Augustus born 7th October 1880 and he and his half brother

Robert Stanley Laxen were baptised together on the 5th May 1881. In September 1882, Annie and Robert Bullock had a daughter Maggie Elizabeth. The Laxen/Bullock family remained at the Stonemasons until 1890 when they moved to the New Inn in Red Lion Street where Robert was the publican for a year. In 1900, Henry Fenn Laxen, the son of Annie and Richard Laxen died in the South African War when he was twenty six years old, and a tablet erected in his memory is to be seen on a wall in St Michael's church in Aylsham.

The Stonemasons has existed in Millgate since 1846 and is one of the few public houses remaining in Aylsham which is patronised not only by local residents, but those from nearby areas who enjoy a game of pool and darts matches. An annual Robert Burns celebration night was instigated by John (Jock) Cairncross, the Scottish publican from 1975 until his death in 1995 and this event has been carried on in subsequent years.

The Stonemasons Quoits Team 1911.
(By permission of Pauline Hagon)
Top row left to right:- Bob Gould, unknown, Albert Long, Dick Long, F. Ducker, G. Goodwin, Mike Ducker Sen.
Middle row:- Tom Rendell, G. Oliver (publican of the Stonemasons) Wymer, Sid Kerrison, G. Lake
Front row:- G Wright, unknown, Mike Ducker, Jack Wymer

The Stonemasons Arms 1970.
(By permission of the Aylsham Association)

The Stonemasons 1995.

THE ANCHOR INN

PUBLICAN		OWNER	
John Jennings	1781-1798	Robert Parmeter	1780
Joseph Dean	1795	Anne Lungley	1791
James Marsh	1795-1797		
John Harriman	1798-1804		
William Wilson	1805-1830	Francis Parmeter	1833
William Mash, farmer + builder	1836-1846	Messrs. Bircham	1833-1878
James Fitt	1850-1856		
Robert Easton	1858-1865		
Thomas Wright + water bailiff	1868-1877		
Thomas Read	1877-1888	Steward & Patteson	1878-1962
James Tight + fish curer	1890-1900		
Ernest Clarke + fish curer	1904-1937		
Clifford Spink	1937-1961		

The Anchor closed in 1961

The site of the Anchor Inn in Millgate possibly dates to the 1600s, but so far no documentary evidence has been found to substantiate this theory. The earliest documentation is in the will of Henry Wymarke made in 1746. In this will he left property on this site to his two daughters. One daughter Hannah, the wife of John Webster, surrendered the property in 1753 to Thomas Spurrell, a miller of Aylsham. Robert Parmeter a miller and flour merchant, bought the property from the executors of Thomas Spurrell in 1771. At this date, it was described as two messuages adjoining and situated near the bridge in Millgate Street. These messuages were occupied by Hammond Beaton, John Beaton and John Smith and had yards and gardens. The sale also included a meadow, called Pond Meadow, a further meadowland on the east of the River Bure and other land in the area.

Robert Parmeter not only owned the Aylsham Mill, but built the maltings in Millgate in 1771 and bought other properties and land in and around Aylsham. He invested money in the Navigation Company which was formed to make a canal, allowing wherries to sail from Cromer and Yarmouth with their cargoes to the Aylsham Mill. This canal was completed in 1779 and the wherries sailed from Cromer and Yarmouth to Thurne and up the River Bure, passing through locks at Coltishall, Buxton, Lammas, Oxnead and Burgh and on to the Aylsham mill pool. It may have been this increase in trade that made Robert Parmeter convert the messuages in Millgate into an inn in 1781 as a business enterprise. The wherrymen who brought their cargoes to the mill would certainly have welcomed a venue where they could obtain liquid refreshment and a simple meal, just as later many of them were customers of the nearby Royal Oak in Dunkirk. When Robert Parmeter died in 1791, he left the Anchor to his daughter Anne Lungley, the wife of Isaac Lungley, a farmer in Boxford, Suffolk. Anne Lungley continued to own the Anchor for many years, but did not live there and employed publicans to run the establishment for her.

In 1833, Francis Parmeter, the son of Robert Parmeter the younger and a beer brewer of Booton Hall near to Aylsham, sold the Anchor to William Bircham, a Reepham brewer. Francis Parmeter had acquired the inn from his relative Anne Lungley and it was again sold in 1878 to Steward and Patteson, the Norwich and Ely brewers. The sale notice describes the property as containing a large parlour, a good tap and bar, stone paved cellar, kitchen and store room. Four bedrooms and two attics, yard in rear with gates to road, in which is stabling for about twenty horses, a skittle ground and a good garden bounded by the river. Steward and Patteson retained ownership of the inn until 1961 when it was closed and offered for sale by public auction.

The auction of the sale of the Anchor Inn by Steward and Patteson took place on the 15th January 1962 at the Aylsham Town Hall. It was referred to in the sale catalogue as a detached riverside residence, situated in Millgate Street, half a mile from Aylsham Market Place and built of red brick with a Dutch gable and a tiled roof.

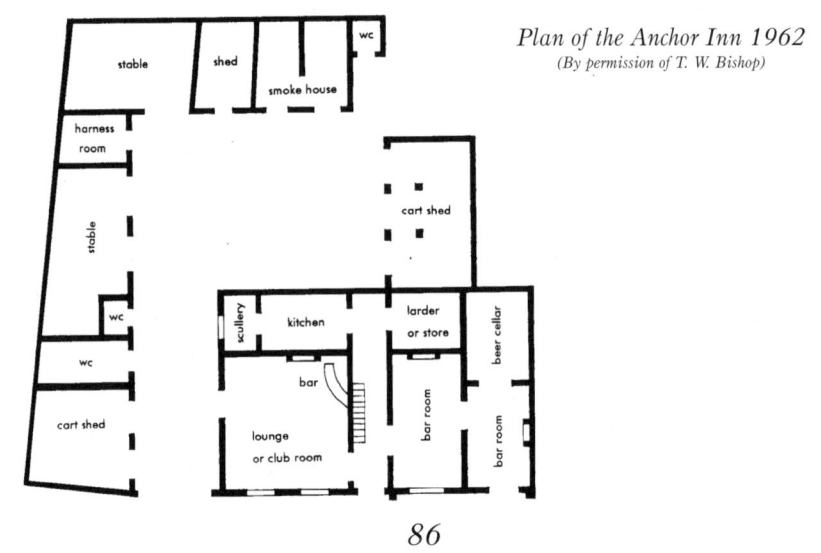

Plan of the Anchor Inn 1962
(By permission of T. W. Bishop)

The property was also advertised as extending to over one acre of ground with extensive outbuildings. The catalogue for this sale is of interest as it gives details of the interior of the former inn. The ground floor had an entrance hall with a quarry tile floor, a sitting room, 18ft. 2 in. x 16ft. 10 in., a dining room, 17ft. 6 in. x 10ft. 8 in. and a study 12ft. 6in. x 8ft. 3 in. Other rooms on this floor were a kitchen, scullery, larder and a cellar which was built as a lean-to addition at the rear of the building. The first floor had a landing, and three bedrooms, with the main bedroom 18ft. x 17ft, the other two were of a smaller size. This floor also had a boxroom, bathroom and a separate W.C. and a further floor above had a landing and two bedrooms both of which were 19ft.x 6in. x 11ft. From these details it is possible to form some idea of the size of the former Anchor Inn.

Early photographs of the Anchor Inn, show two doors that led directly from the road into the building and these doors would have been there before the two messuages were converted into one. After 1962, the door on the right was removed and the entrance filled in with bricks. To the right and close to the bridge there were two small thatched roof cottages which at some time were demolished and a single one storey building erected in their place. Changes have also been made to the building since 1962 with the installation of windows that had previously been infilled and a third dormer window has been added between the two original ones in the attic to provide light on the landing. Because the Anchor was in close proximity to the River Bure, an underground cellar was impossible as it would have been prone to flooding and the cellar was therefore a lean-to adjoining the back of the building with a flagstone floor and the barrels kept on trestles.

Although the inn dates back to the late 1700s and continued until 1961, it had very few publicans in those years. They must have been content as many put in long years of service and apart from the responsibilities of running a public house, some had other occupations. William Mash is a prime example as he was also a farmer and builder. He was born in 1800 and had his own farm at the age of twenty three. He may also have bought property for in 1831, he sold a dwelling house which he owned to Thomas Stoneham, an Aylsham baker. Three years later, he inherited some property behind Red Lion Street and rented this to Jonathan Burrell.

The Anchor Inn on the left 1900s.

Former Anchor Inn 1962.

In 1836, William Mash became the publican of the Anchor Inn and continued farming by buying or renting land. He also began acquiring property and in 1845, he either erected cottages or renovated those already there on a site in Millgate. These are numbers 2, 4, and 6 and the initials of he and his wife Elizabeth and the date are on the front facade of one cottage. This building enterprise was followed in the same year by the building of six cottages on land that he owned at the end of Millgate and in 1848, he built two houses on the same site. The cottages have a plaque with WEM 1845 and between the two semi detached houses picked out in small pebbles are the initials WEM and the date 1848. These cottages and houses are known as Mash's Row. William Mash left the Anchor in 1846 and died three years later at the early age of forty nine and is buried in St Michael's churchyard. His widow, Elizabeth Hayne Mash was left with two young children, Katherine aged six and Henry Brett who was only four years old and they continued to live in Millgate. A more detailed account of the Mash family is to be found in the *Millgate* book, published by the Aylsham Local History Society.

James Fitt was the publican from 1850 until 1858 and during his time, the Aylsham Aquatic Club was formed on the 9th May 1851. This club met regularly at the inn with Samuel Parmeter as the President and Dr. Fred Smith as the Commodore and the aims of the club were to promote rowing matches on the River Bure. Two other publicans, James Tight 1890-1900 and Ernest Clarke from 1904-1937, were fish curers. The smokehouse at the rear of the Anchor had formerly been a cottage and later a bakery. Herrings delivered from Yarmouth were slotted on to rods and placed high in the building and smoked from a wood fire at ground level. This smokehouse fell into disrepair in later years when it was no longer used and it has now been restored by the present owner.

The Great Flood of 1912 caused considerable damage to the locks on the Navigation Canal which was near to the Anchor and considered too expensive to repair. Eventually, the wherries ceased coming to Aylsham Mill and the railways took over the transportation of goods. The wherrymen, who had patronised the Anchor and the Royal Oak in Dunkirk were customers of the past, but others took their place and these were the soldiers billeted in the Maltings and at the Staithe in World War I. During World War II, the forces stationed in or near

Painting of the Anchor Inn 1850
(By permission of T. W. Bishop)

Bridge House 1995.

to Aylsham were also visitors to the inn as well as the railway men from the North Aylsham station. This railway line was closed in 1958 and the station was demolished soon after and affected the Anchor Inn business. Its viability was in question, but it continued for another four years until Steward and Patteson decided to close it down and sell the premises. Many visitors to Aylsham make a point of seeing the historic water mill which can be viewed from the bridge in Millgate, but few will be aware that the house on the opposite side of the road, now named Bridge House, was once an inn.

THE ROYAL OAK

PUBLICAN		OWNER	
Matthew Howes	1843		
Thomas Lovell	1845		
William Lomax	1858		
James Wright	1863-1865	Youngs & Crawshay	1863-1865
Thomas Wright	1865		
Robert Felstead	1865-1869		
Edward Brown + Robert Felstead	1872-1875	Youngs, Crawshay & Co.	1872-1938
John Atkinson	1883		
William Atkinson	1883-1888		
John Crane	1890-1896		
Albert Charles Pumphrey + carpenter	1900-1938		
Anna Elizabeth Pumphrey	1938		

The Royal Oak closed in 1938

The Royal Oak was a small public house, sometimes referred to as beerhouse, which was situated in Dunkirk and close to the Navigation Canal in the northern part of Aylsham. It was established in 1843 and became the venue for local residents, agricultural workers from nearby farms and the wherrymen who brought cargoes to the Aylsham Mill. In August 1912, the Royal Oak suffered severe flooding as did many buildings in the surrounding area. After a drying out period, business resumed, but with the later decline of the wherries, the wherrymen were no longer patrons. During the 1914-1918 war, soldiers billeted at the Staithe and in Millgate were frequent visitors to this public house.

From 1900-1938, the publican of the Royal Oak was Albert Charles Pumphrey, and the owners were Youngs, Crawshay & Co. Only beer and ale were sold and the barrels were kept in a lean-to on the right hand side of the building as an underground cellar was impossible due to the level of the water table in this area. The beer and ale was drawn from barrels into an earthenware jug from which glasses were filled. Apart from purchasing beer and ale, customers could also buy tobacco for their pipes or roll up cigarettes. The favourite brand was Dark Shag, kept in a jar and sold in small quantities. Also obtainable was a simple meal of bread, cheese and pickled onions.

The Royal Oak had only one bar with access through the front door beyond a small forecourt which had wooden rails for the tethering of horses. On this forecourt a ten foot pole displayed a sign of an oak tree in full leaf. On the left of the building, a wide entrance allowed carts to be driven into a rear yard. The bar had wooden benches on three sides of the room with a long table placed in the centre. On the right hand side wall, there was a dartboard and the end wall had a fireplace where logs and coal were burned. The flagstone floor was covered with a layer of sand and every morning this was swept and sieved to remove the cigarette ends. The sieved sand was then sprinkled back on the floor and fresh sand added. Besides the bar on the ground floor there were three other rooms and a kitchen for the use of the publican. Stairs led to the first floor which had three bedrooms and two other small rooms or storage spaces. All the rooms in the Royal Oak were lit with candles and oil lamps before gas and electricity came to Aylsham.

In his time as the publican, Albert Charles Pumphrey also worked as a carpenter. His first wife died in 1893 at the age of 33 years and he later re-married. He died in February 1938 aged 76 years and was buried in Aylsham cemetery. His widow Anna Elizabeth, carried on at the Royal Oak for a few months until it closed at the end of 1938. She retired to The Oaks in Dunkirk and died at the age of 81 years.

After the closure of the Royal Oak, the building was sold and converted into two separate cottages and later became one dwelling named the 'Maiden's Bower'; this name can be traced back to 1687. On the 10th December 1687, Thomas Empson a grocer of Aylsham, made his will and part of it is reproduced.
'Also to son William, 7 acres lying by the Waterie Lane leading to Tuttington and abutting land late of Thomas Baker, Gentleman.
Also to him 3 acres of land adjoining the 7 acres and called Great - Kirkmere.
To daughter Anne after wife's decease my messuage and land I bought of James Allen and James Hargrave; also my messuage and land in Aylsham and a meadow called Maiden's Bower, lying by Waterie Lane; also 2 butchers stalls and a shop called the 'Wooll-Crosse' standing in the market place of Aylsham'.

Further information on the Maiden's Bower comes from a document of 1771 in which part of the estate of Thomas Spurrell was sold to Thomas Harvey, a wheelwright. This document states:-
'All that messuage situate in Millgate Street in Aylesham next the King's Highway leading to the bridge on the part of the west, and

the street or way leading to the water mill on the north part, with yard pump and garden to the same belonging. And also the barn and stable adjoining the said messuage, containing by estimation, 1 rood more or less and also that close arable land called or known by the name of Maiden's Bower'.

The estate of Thomas Harvey was sold to Robert Harvey in 1823 and two years later Francis Parmeter purchased the Maiden's Bower land. It would appear from all this information that the present road known as Dunkirk was formerly known as Waterie Lane and before the Navigation Canal was built, this area was meadows and farm land. In later years houses and bungalows were built in Dunkirk, and by the 1960s the surrounding land had been developed as an industrial area.

The Royal Oak.
(By permission of Alan Rowlands)

The Maidens Bower formerly the Royal Oak in Dunkirk.

AYLSHAM'S VANISHED INNS AND PUBLIC HOUSES

Apart from the twenty inns or public houses which have been written about, there are six more named as being in Aylsham. These are the Butcher's Arms, Globe, Maid's Head, Castle, Griffin and the Fox and little is known of the first four. All that has been found are a few names and dates, but as they are a part of Aylsham's history, they should be mentioned.

Edward Pinchin is named at the Globe in 1689 and was succeeded by Widow Wright in 1700. At the Castle, Joseph Allen in 1694, followed by Widow Allen in 1700. The Maid's Head had Edward Rumbull in 1689 and he is also listed at the Unicorn in the same year. No information has been discovered regarding the Butcher's Arms. More is known of the Griffin where the publican was Richard Tennant 1688-1691. He brewed beer at the Griffin and supplied the churchwardens of St. Michael's church with a barrel of beer in 1688 to celebrate the proclamation of King William III. Richard Tennant was followed by John Cannell in 1700 and Jonathan Scottow in 1727.

The Griffin was owned in 1687 by Thomas Empson, a wealthy grocer of Aylsham. An extract from his will is as follows:-
'To son Samuel, a messuage called the Griffin with yards, garden, orchard, barn and stables, with the copper and brewing vessels and all other household stuff therein.
To son William, land and a messuage wherein I now dwell with yard, barn, stable and candle house with a piece of ground called the Ollands lying between the lands of the Angel to the north and the through peece also the Ollands on the south, and the common way to the east. William is to have ingress and egress through the Griffin and the thoroughfare called Ollands, and liberty to draw and fetch water from the pump in the Griffin yard. William and his heirs must pay Samuel half the charges of keeping the pump in repair.'

The location of the Griffin has been impossible to find with the changes of names and land since the 1600s. The sites of the Butcher's Arms, Globe, Maid's Head and Castle are also unknown. It is possible, and a speculative idea, that the names of these five inns were changed at a later date, as was the King's Head to the New Inn in 1791.

The Fox was a small public house in Fox's Loke, a narrow lane leading off the Cawston Road and the earliest date found is 1839. John

Porrett was the publican and owner and died on the 29th October 1840 aged sixty years, and four years after the death of his thirty eight year old wife Susan. Both are buried in St. Michael's churchyard. Robert Herring was the publican from 1843 until 1846. Bircham & Son acquired the property in 1846. It is not known how long this small public house continued, but it has since been demolished and all traces of it have disappeared.

INN AND PUBLIC HOUSE SIGNS

The first signs for inns, taverns and public houses were a direct result of the Roman occupation when the Romans used signs to depict the trades and occupations of citizens. In 1393, Richard II ordered publicans to display signs on their buildings and it is from this date that they developed. The names given to these establishments are taken from various sources and were consistent throughout the country. In origin, they were principally heraldic, religious, historical, nautical, floral, mammalia or connected with Royalty or Royal events. Some were derived from the trades and crafts of a particular area.

Early signs were painted by local craftsmen and in later years by artists employed by breweries. These craftsmen and artists brought their own interpretations to the painted images and the signs were either displayed on a tall pole at the boundary or were hung from a bracket projecting across the road. Some later signs did not have a visual image and had only the name of the inn or public house, many of which were on a plain board attached to the building.

Of the four remaining public houses in Aylsham, only three have a painted sign; these are the Unicorn, the Feathers and the Stonemasons. The sign that the Black Boys once had disappeared many years ago, and has never been replaced. Many of Aylsham's former inns and public houses also had signs, but those that are known as painted images were the White Horse, the Anchor and Royal Oak; the others it would appear had lettered signs. These signs like many in the country would have been derived from traditional sources which are detailed below.

UNICORN
The sign of the Unicorn is derived from the Royal Coat of Arms, which depicts a white horse with a horn on the forehead. The Unicorn is mythological in concept and was adopted as a symbol by the

crusaders. It became a heraldic symbol and many inns adopted it as a sign.

HALF MOON
The Half Moon is the crescent moon in chivalric heraldry and was the ensign of the Turks. It may have entered European heraldry at the time of the crusades.

SWAN
A sign derived from a heraldic symbol. In some localities it is taken from swans who inhabit a nearby river, but it is also known as an emblem of innocence.

FEATHERS
The three feathers was a device of the Black Prince and later represented the amorial plumes of any succeeding Prince of Wales.

DOG
This is thought to traditionally represent a dog pretending to be a man and also indicated that an inn had changed ownership. Hence the expression, 'An old dog in new clothing'.

ANGEL
Inns named the Angel were of religious origin. Some Angel signs showed an image of St Michael carrying a sword and shield.

BULL
The sign of the bull is from a medieval heraldic source. There were many English inns with the name from 1533. It was sometimes named from the monastic bulla, the seal of an abbot's licence.

KING'S HEAD
A favourite sign for the King's Head was an image of Henry VIII or Charles II; later these signs depicted succeeding male monarchs. Some signs however had as their source the King of Hearts taken from a playing card.

NEW INN
The term New Inn, generally denotes the change of title from a previous establishment. The New Inn also took the name from a time when monasteries administered the premises.

CROSS KEYS
The Cross Key sign is taken from ecclesiastical heraldry. One key is of gold and the other of silver which are presented in saltire. Their symbol denotes the power of Christ conferred on St Peter.

STAR
This sign has connections not only with heraldry, but also with the early days of sailing.

RED LION
The Red Lion was the emblem of John of Gaunt, the Duke of Lancaster. There are many Red Lion inns throughout the country, but the Red Lion in Aylsham had a particular connection to John of Gaunt.

SHIP
In the middle ages, inns were the commercial centres for merchants and traders with a sea connection. The sign of the Ship began as a chivalric charge and was incorporated into the armorial bearings of merchant companies. The sign has continued in seafaring ports and oddly enough was the name of one of Aylsham's inns situated far from a sea port, or near to a local river.

WHITE HART
The sign of the White Hart depicts a white stag wearing a gold collar and chain. It is said to date to Alexander the Great, who captured a white stag and placed a gold collar around its neck. Richard II adopted this emblem in his coat of arms.

WHITE HORSE
This inn sign is thought to have developed from Saxon times and from the House of Hanover in the years after 1714. The emblem is also connected to the White Horse cut out in the chalk hills of Wiltshire and Berkshire.

ANCHOR
The sign of the anchor has religious connotations and also connections to river and sea going vessels.

ROYAL OAK
The sign of the Royal Oak depicts a large oak tree in full leaf. This

name given to inns and public houses commemorates Charles II's escape from capture in 1651 following the Battle of Worcester, when it is said he hid in an oak tree at Boscobel, near Shifnal in Shropshire. After the restoration, Charles II's birthday on the 29th May, was celebrated as Oakapple Day in Aylsham.

GRIFFIN
A name derived from heraldry. A mythical monster, part lion, part eagle and supposed to typify strength and vigilance. The Griffin is represented in heraldry with the body, tail and hind legs of a lion, the head, neck, breast, forelegs and wings of an eagle with ears forward pointing.

BUTCHER'S ARMS
Thought to derive from the formation of the Butcher's Company, but many signs were derived from local butchers.

GLOBE
A name which dates from the reign of Elizabeth I with the circumnavigation of the world. The name is also associated with the Globe theatre in London where Shakespeare's plays were performed in the 1600s.

MAID'S HEAD
Dates from Tudor times and refers to Elizabeth I as the virgin queen.

CASTLE
A title derived from the importance of castles built by landowners as a defence against invasion. Also taken from Castile, indicating the sale of Spanish wines.

BREWERS AND BREWERIES

There were a number of brewers and malsters in Aylsham from the 1600s until the late 1800s. Brewing was almost certainly carried on in the town prior to the 17th century, and many large houses and farms from nearby areas had brewhouses to produce ale for family consumption. Many Aylsham residents in the 1800s also brewed beer in their homes from malt and hops bought from Bullock's malt house in Millgate. This home made beer was bottled into 2 pint stone bottles, left to mature and placed in sunlight to produce a sparkling brew. Cider was also another domestic beverage and made each autumn from the apples of local orchards. Domestic wine was produced from the fruits of elderberries, raspberries, redcurrants and blackcurrants. Other wines were made from root vegetables, such as carrots, parsnips and potatoes. Sloe gin and cherry whisky were made, but few could afford the spirits required and these spiritous drinks were a luxury reserved for Christmas.

Although there were early brewhouses in the town, their locations are relatively unknown, but descriptions have been found in a number of documents. The earliest is in 1607 when Margaret Chosell had a messuage with le Brewhouse and Backhouse and other buildings containing 10 spaces called Hourdardes, with close and le yard adjacent. In 1610, Thomas and Emma Leoman owned a messuage called Silks and Mansers with a mill house, brewhouse, an orchard and garden, a croft and a little pightle. William and Christina Orwell in 1615, owned a messuage with gardens, a malt house, other outbuildings, an orchard, a hempland and le backyard.

Edward or Edmund Reve in 1620 had a pightle called Stones Howse and a built up messuage called Halls with le brewhouse. In his will of 1639, Edmund Wattes, a wealthy baker in Aylsham, left many properties and land to his wife and family. An inventory after his death lists one of his properties as a messuage with three main rooms, furnished with beds, tables, chairs, stools and chests, a hall, a kitchen and buttery. The property also had a bakehouse, brewhouse, corn chamber, lumber chamber, two barns and a stable. One copper, brewing vessels and tubs are also listed, indicating that brewing was carried out on a small scale.

In October 1663, James Allen a beer brewer of Aylsham, made his will and left messuages or tenements that he owned in Marsham to his daughter Sarah and her heirs. His wife Margarott was left land to be passed on and divided between their daughters Mary, Margarott and Susan when they reached the age of twenty three years. His wife also retained all other properties to be passed to their sons James, John and Thomas on attaining their individual twenty fourth year.

The will of Richard Greenwood, vintner of Aylsham in 1666 and the inventory made on the 10th May 1666 after his death shows that he was a beer brewer. Richard Greenwood had either lived in a very substantial sized house or in one of the larger Aylsham inns. The inventory details the contents of thirteen rooms, various outbuildings, stables, brewhouse, backhouse and cellars.
The latter are written of as follows:-
'In the beer seller-
Fower barrells of strong beer.
Three Alestooles.
In the wyne seller-
One pipe of Canary Sack.
One parte of a hogshead of Malago sack.
One hogshead of White wyne.
Some ullages of Rennish wyne and muskadine.
In the brewhouse and backhouse-
Seven beer hogsheads.
Six new beer barrells.
Six new halfe barrells.
Two bucking tubbs.
Two weighing killers.
Three hooks and some lumber.'

There were also several brewers in White Hart Street, Jonathan Ulph in 1737, Henry Poll from 1839-1868 and William Cooper 1872-1879, who was also a maltster. In Millgate two brewers are known; John Freeman in 1850 and Charles Cooper, described as a beer retailer and brewer in 1869. Hungate Street had Ezra Pilgrim, brewer and maltster in 1850 and William Smart in 1854. There were other maltsters in Aylsham who were not brewers; one was William Rannalls 1725-1730 and another was Robert Parmeter, who built the maltings in Millgate in 1771.

From the mid 1800s, the inns and public houses in Aylsham had been bought up by brewery companies from private owners. The ownership changed over the years with the merger of small Norfolk breweries or in a take over by larger companies. It was profitable for a brewery firm to own public houses as an outlet for their products without competition. The companies entered into contract with other suppliers for products which they were unable to provide; these were mainly spirits, wines and various brands of stout. The details of the brewery companies who owned inns and public houses in Aylsham are very complex, but are briefly detailed below.

THE COLTISHALL BREWERY
This brewery had been built up by Robert Hawes, who was one of the first brewers to own inns and public houses and owned the Bull Inn in Aylsham. He died in March 1841 at the early age of forty eight and left his young widow with three children, the eldest three years, another was one year old and the youngest only four months.

The Brewery, although small in scale, was very profitable and the Hawes family enjoyed a high standard of living and was amongst the richest in Coltishall. Their home at the Old House was surrounded by brewery buildings and had two malthouses. Opposite was a stable block accommodating twelve Shire horses, which were used to haul drays loaded with beer barrels to public houses at Catton, Blofield, Ludham, North Walsham, Cromer and Aylsham. Other barrels were transported by wherries along river routes to their destinations.

After the death of Robert Hawes, the Coltishall Brewery Estate was auctioned in September 1841. Besides the brewery buildings and the two malthouses, the sale also included fifty three inns and public houses. The buyers are not known, but some of the estate appears to have been acquired by the brewery firm of Steward & Patteson.

BULLARD & SONS LTD.
The Anchor Brewery, St Miles Bridge in Norwich was founded in 1837 with a partnership of Bullard and Watts. The brewery expanded considerably and in 1845 owned or leased thirty licensed houses; by 1861 this number had risen to eighty. Richard Bullard was administrating the company by 1848 and after his death at the age of fifty six in 1864, he was succeeded by his son, later Sir Harry Bullard. In 1864, the brewery became a limited company and owned 280 public houses, leased 161 and owned 7 malthouses.

In Bullard's expansion, they took over a number of small breweries including the Rock Brewery of Eye in Suffolk in 1897, Bidwell &

Co. of Thetford in 1924, Hogg & Seppings 1928 and Youngs, Crawshay & Youngs Ltd. in 1958. Bullard & Sons were taken over by Watney Mann Ltd. in 1964 when they owned 530 tied houses throughout East Anglia. Brewing ceased at the Anchor Brewery in 1968 and the buildings were demolished and the majority of the site cleared during the 1970s.

TRUNCH BREWERY LTD.
The Trunch Brewery was formed in 1803 by the Primrose family and by 1865, William Primrose had extended the malting and brewing business. In 1869, the brewery was being administered by Philip S. Primrose, who was succeeded by Mrs B. N. Primrose between 1888 and 1904. The brewery then passed to W. D. Churchill, but by 1912, Edward Woodyatt was in charge and his successor was Cuthbert B. Smith in 1921. By 1952, the Trunch Brewery Ltd. had been acquired by Morgan & Co.

WATNEY MANN AND NORWICH BREWERY
In 1952, Morgan & Co. took over the Trunch Brewery which had nine public houses, but was itself taken over in 1961 by two rivals, Bullards and Steward & Patteson. In this takeover, 450 public houses were divided between the two companies and the Trunch Brewery was sold to Watney Mann. A separate company Watney Mann (East Anglia Ltd.) was formed in 1963 to operate the brewery. This was extensively re-built between 1969 and 1971. A year later in June 1972, Watney Mann was taken over by Grand Metropolitan Hotels and in 1976, the name of Watney Mann was changed to the Norwich Brewery Co.Ltd.

MORGAN BREWERY CO. LTD.
This brewery was in King Street, Norwich and was established in 1720, but there is evidence that brewing had been carried on at this site in earlier centuries. The Tompson family were the brewers in 1720 and continued until 1845, when they sold the brewery and fifty four public houses to John Brandram and Walter Morgan. This brewery company expanded and Walter Morgan was replaced by his brother Henry. It became a limited company in March 1887 and owned 106 public houses and leased 82 others.

The company took over a number of small breweries including the Crown Brewery of Chatteris in 1889, Bourke and Elwes at Grimston in 1890 and William Cannes Wymondham Brewery in 1894. Further expansions continued with the purchase of the Cozens-Hardy & Sons, Letheringsett Brewery in 1896. In 1900, Morgan's purchased the Elijah Eyre's Lady Bridge Brewery in King's Lynn, followed by E & G Morse's Crown Brewery at Lowestoft in 1936. All these acquisitions gave Morgan's a total of 600 public houses in East Anglia. In 1961, Morgan's was the victim of a take over bid from Bullard and Steward & Patteson and the tied estate of public houses was divided between these two companies.

STEWARD & PATTESON
This company was one of the most successful in East Anglia and at its peak not only owned breweries, but also a number of inns and public houses. Many of those that they owned from the 1800s until the latter half of the 1900s were in Aylsham. William Steward 1760-1841 was a merchant and invested in brewing and public houses, which by 1830 extended from East Anglia into Kent.

In 1792 John Patteson, a beer brewer, acquired the small Pockthorpe Norwich Brewery owned by Charles Greeves and later bought two more Norwich breweries belonging to James Beevor and Jehosophat Postle. John Patteson's son, John Stanisford Patteson, succeeded his father and developed the brewing business. John Patteson retired in 1820 and a co-partnership was formed between John Stanisford Patteson, William Steward, Ambrose Harbord Steward, Timothy Steward and his son also named Timothy. John Stanisford Patteson and Timothy Steward the younger, were responsible for the management and production of the brewery. The merger of the Stewards with the Pattesons was fortunate for the latter, as the former contributed two thirds of the brewery capital. In 1831 George Morse, another leading Norwich brewer, amalgamated with Steward & Patteson and brought the ownership of another seventy seven public houses to the company. A further merger occurred in 1837 with the Norwich brewery of Finch & Co.

World War I and World War II had an adverse effect on Steward & Patteson with the scarcity of ingredients for the production of beer and a reduced work force, many of whom had been conscripted into the armed forces. Steward & Patteson however managed to survive and supplied the public houses and inns with beer during these difficult times. The company sustained losses during these periods, but made a good recovery.

In August 1949 Steward & Patteson acquired the brewery company of Soames & Co. of Spalding and, in January 1957, bought a further sixty six public houses in Lincolnshire. They continued to expand with the purchase of East Anglian Brewers of Ely. This purchase gave them a total of 1,250 public houses.

The decline of Steward & Patteson as one of the most powerful brewery companies began in 1961 when they closed and sold the public houses which they owned in East Anglia. In 1967, Steward & Patteson sold over 1,000 licensed properties to Watney Mann, and this was the end of an era for a company that had operated successfully for 170 years.

YOUNGS, CRAWSHAY & YOUNGS
This company owned the Crown Brewery in King Street, Norwich. John Youngs was brewer in St Ethelreds parish in 1807 and was in partnership with Jonathan Davey. The partnership was dissolved in 1841 and the firm traded as Youngs & Co. until 1830 when William Burt became a partner. John Youngs son, also called John, developed the business and went into partnership with Richard Crawshay in 1851. Richard Crawshay had purchased a brewery in St Stephen's Street in Norwich from Isaac Johnson, which he sold when he became John Youngs partner. The firm traded as Crawshay & Youngs or Youngs Crawshay, operating from the brewery in King Street. At a later date, the younger brother of John Youngs joined the partnership and they traded as Youngs, Crawshay & Youngs becoming a limited company in November 1897. They were the smallest of the Norwich brewers, but nevertheless owned 250 public houses by 1958. In that year they were taken over by Bullard & Sons, after which the brewery closed and was later demolished.

BIRCHAM & SONS
This firm was founded by William Bircham, a Reepham brewer. In 1833 he was in partnership with Francis Parmeter, a beer brewer of Booton Hall near Aylsham. The firm traded as Bircham & Parmeter until 1850. By 1865, Francis Parmeter had withdrawn from the company which was then known as Bircham & Sons. On the 8th June 1878, the brewery with its fifty two licensed public houses was auctioned and bought by Steward & Patteson, Finch & Co. of Norwich.

WILLIAM HARDY

William Hardy purchased Hagen's Brewery at Letheringsett in November 1780. By 1838, this brewery owned nine tied houses and the business was extended by William's son, also called William who died in 1842. The estate passed to his nephew, William Hardy Cozens who under the conditions of his uncle's will, changed his surname to Cozens-Hardy. He expanded the brewery firm, and by 1888 it was trading as W. H. Cozens-Hardy & Son. William Cozens-Hardy died in 1895 and the company was purchased by Morgan & Co. in 1896.

REFERENCES

AYSHAM ARCHIVES
Poor Rate Assessment Books 1723-1900.
Register of Meeting Houses 1756.
Aylsham Dissenter Meeting Houses Register Dn/Dis/4/2 1824-1855.
Aylsham St. Michael's Churchyard Survey.
Aylsham & District Almanacks 1884-1906.
Account Book Light Infantry Volunteers 1803.
Admissions to the Workhouse 1803-1836.
Register of Apprentices 1824.
Burial Board Book 1885-1905.
Bastardy Book 1808.

NORFOLK RECORD OFFICE
Norfolk Chronicle and Norwich Gazette 1774-1784.
Bury and Norwich Post 1790-1794.
Norwich Mercury 1794.
Aylsham Lancaster Manor Court Book 1648-1664, NRO NRS 16615.
Aylsham Lancaster Manor Court Book 1664-1704 NRO NRS 16616.
Aylsham Papers of Joseph Clover NRO MC 119.
Will of Jonathan Ulph NRO NCC 6G (MF 97).
Probate Inventory of Jonathan Ulph NRO NCC INV. 80 E/1.
Alehouse Keepers Recognances C Sch. 1/16 1787-1799 NRO MC 119/25.
Will of Thomas Empson 1687 NRO ANW No. 180 MF/RO 466/8.
Will of Robert Hall 1668-9 F 319 MF/RO 332/2.

DIRECTORIES
Universal British Directory Vol. II pp 83-85.
White's Norfolk Directories 1846-1890.
Kelly's Norfolk Directories 1853-1937.
Harrods's Norfolk Directories 1863-1877.
Pigot & Co. Norfolk Directories 1830-1879.
Post Office Norfolk Directories 1869-1879.
Riche's Norfolk Directory 1843.
Hunt & Co. Norfolk Directory 1850.
Melville & Co's. Directory 1856.

AYLSHAM LOCAL HISTORY SOCIETY PUBLICATIONS
Journal Volume 1 No's 3 and 9 1986-1987.
Journal Volume 2 No's 6 and 12 1989-1990
Journal Volume 3 No's 3, 4, 6, 8, 9, 11 and 12 1991-1993
Journal Volume 4 No. 3 1994.
Aylsham in 1821, Occasional Paper No. 1.
Aylsham in the Seventeenth Century, published 1988.
Millgate, Aylsham, 1993.
James Wright Map of 1893 published by the ALHS 1994.
Memories of Aylsham, William Frederick Starling 2000.

TITLE DEEDS
Half Moon Cottage, courtesy of Jack and Mary Edmonds.
The Ship, courtesy of Jill Kemp.

BOOKS
Batchelor, D., *The English Inn,* Batsford 1963.
Brewery Society, *Inn Signs - Their History and Meaning* 1969.
Clark, Peter., *The English Alehouse, A Social History 1200-1830* Longman 1983.
Cox, Barrie., *English Inn and Tavern Names*, The Centre for English Studies, University of Nottingham.
Gaunt, W., *Old Inns of England,* Batsford 1958.
Gourvish, Terry., *Norfolk Beers from English Barley,* Centre of East Anglia Studies, University of East Anglia 1987.
Jackson, Michael, editor., *The World Guide to Beer,* Mitchell Beazley 1977.
Malster, Robert., *Wherries and Waterways,* Terence Dalton Ltd. 1971.
Monckton, H.A., *A History of English Ale and Beer,* The Bodley Head 1966.
Richardson, John., *The Local Historians Encyclopedia,* Historical Publications Ltd. 1986.
Robinson, Bruce and Tony Gregory., *Celtic Fire and Roman Rule,* Poppyland 1987.
Sapwell, John., *A History of Aylsham,* Rigby Printing Company Ltd. 1960.

INDEX

Abbot's Hall 5
Abbot's House 5
Abbott, Mrs 51
Abbott, Sampson 5
Aegal's Ham 1
Aegel 1
Ailesham 1
Allen, James 93, 102
Allen, John 60
Allen, Joseph 96
Allen, M.A. heirs 66
Allen, Maria 66
Allen, Thomas 36
Anchor Brewery 104
Anchor Inn 84-90
Anchor Sign 100
Anderson 23
Angel Close 45
Angel Inn, 45-47
Angel Sign 99
Angling Club 24
Aquatic Club 89
Assemblies 16
Assembly Room 16, 21
Atkins 80
Atkinson, John 92
Atkinson, William 92
Austin, Watts 60, 64
Austin, William George 79
Aylesham 1
Aylsham 1
Aylsham and Buxton Rowing Club 62
Aylsham Archives 1, 38, 77
Aylsham Association 16
Aylsham Manor 43, 44

Back, George 36
Bailey, Sidney 71
Baker, Harriet 64
Baker, Miles Augustus 60, 64
Ball, John and Jenny 13
Balls, Edward Charles 23
Balls, Harry 23
Barber, William 71
Barclay & Co. 47
Barclay's Bank Ltd 47
Barnard, Eugenie 50
Barnard, Walter 50
Barnes, Fiddy 31
Barnes, Maureen and Ronald 43

Bayfield House 5
Bayfield Matthew 48
Beard, Capt. Richard 13, 19, 20,
                               60, 64, 65
Beard, Margaret 19
Beard, Violet 19, 64
Beasy, Robert 31
Beasy's Rookery 31
Beaton, Hammond 85
Beaton, John 85
Beauchamp Proctor 15
Beck, James 23
Bedder, Ted and June 23
Beeches, The 6
Beeching, Dr. Richard 3
Bell, Thomas 13, 29
Belt Lodge 5
Belt, The 5
Bennet, John 45
Bennet, Thomas Leigh 46
Berry, John 23, 79
Berry, Mary 79
Bircham, John 50
Bircham, Messrs. 48, 97, 107
Bircham, Samuel and Anne 13, 16
Bircham, William & Co. 31, 86
Bircham, William 31, 48, 69, 76, 77
Bird, Elizabeth 66
Bird, George 66
Bird, Joseph 66
Bird, Rebecca 66
Bishop, John 69
Bishop, John Jegon 43
Black Boys 13-22
Bland, Frederick 66
Blickling Hall 4
Blickling Road 4
Blofield's Loke 51
Blyth, William 73
Boer War 41
Bolding, John 23
Bone, Richard R. 60
Boon or Book, Susannah 50
Bowers 70
Bowers Mary 69
Bowers Matilda 70
Bowers Robert 71
Bowers Virtue 71
Bowman, Henry James 43
Bowman, Jul. 48

111

Bowman, Lucy Hulbert 43
Bowyer, Benjamin 36
Bowyer, Mary 36, 37
Boyers, John 70
Brawn, Ex-Sergeant Major 67
Bray, John 13
Breese, James 13
Brent Walker 79
Brett, Benjamin 48
Brewery, The 73
Bridewell 3
Bridge House 91
Briggs, George 71
British Legion 64
Brown, Captain 66
Brown, Edward 92
Brown, Henry 66
Brown, William 69
Buck, Edward Clarence 66
Bull Inn Sign 99
Bull Inn, The 48, 49
Bullard & Sons Ltd. 13, 48, 66, 79, 80, 104
Bullard, Frederick 13
Bullard, Nicholas 69
Bullen, Sarah A. 58
Bullock, Annie Frances 52, 82
Bullock, Robert 50, 52, 79, 82
Bulwer, James 43
Bure House 5
Bure Way 4, 6
Bure, River 3, 62, 85, 87
Burgh Road 37, 45, 47, 51
Burnham Thorpe 16
Burrell, Lucy 55, 56
Burrell, William 55, 56
Burton, John 48
Bush, Benjamin 69
Bush, Mary 69, 76
Bush, Stephen 69
Bushey House 5
Butchers Arms 96
Butchers Arms Sign 101
Butler, James 60
Buttlands 24

Cairncross, John (Jock) 79, 83
Cannell, John 96
Castle Sign 101
Castle, The 96

Cawston Road 3, 4, 20
Cedar House 5
Chalker, Elizabeth 23
Chalker, Matthew Coulfont 23
Chamberlain, Misses 6
Chapel Street 69
Chapman, Fanny 79, 80
Chapman, John 60
Chapman, Richard 79, 80
Chappell, James B. 73
Chappell, James B. Exc. 73
Ching, Wilmot 44
Chosell, Margaret 102
Church Hill 70, 71
Churches 1, 2
Churchwardens Accounts 45
Cinematographic Palace 25
City Sheriff 6
Clare, Robert 45
Clark, George 60
Clarke, Ernest 85
Clarke, Francis C. 13
Clarke, George 58
Clarke, John Secker 13
Clarke, John Secker Excr. 13
Clarke, Richard 13
Clarke, Thomas 36
Claxton, Noah 23
Clements, C 56
Clover, Joseph 79
Coltishall 2
Coltishall Brewery 104
Commercial Road 6
Commissioners Aylsham Navigation 41
Cooke, John Hannant 32, 55
Cooke, Maria 31
Cooke, William 31
Cooper, Charles 103
Cooper, George and Alan 33, 49
Cooper, John 60, 61
Cooper, William 73, 103
Co-Operative Society 19
Cope, Lewis James 13
Copeman & Co. 46, 47
Copeman, George and Thomas 46
Copeman, Mary 50
Copeman, Robert 46
Copeman, William 50
Cornall 62
Corpus Christi College 43

112

Cossor, Robert 48
County Council 4
County Court 41
Courage 33
Cozens-Hardy, W. 50, 108
Cozens-Hardy, W.H. 50, 108
Crane, John 92
Cressy, Thomas 45, 46
Crisp, William 36
Criterian Inns 33
Cromer and Sheringham Operatic Society 65
Cromer 1
Cromer Road 5, 70
Cromwell, Oliver 14
Cross Keys Sign 100
Cross Keys, The 55-57
Crown 10
Cubitt, Robert 23
Cubitt, Widow 23
Curties, James 76
Curtis, W. 66
Custons, Jonathan 69
Cutting, William 36

Dadley, James 31
Danes 1
Davey, John 36
Dazely, Arthur J. 49
De Cole, John 23
Dean of Norwich 43
Dean, Joseph 85
Defoe, Daniel 14
Diamond Jubilee 16
Dickerson, Thomas Martin 36
Diggins, James 58
Dissenter Meeting Houses 26
Dix, Alice 60
Dix, Thomas 60
Dixon, Walter 79
Docking, Ernest William 79
Dodman, Elizabeth 70, 71
Dodman, Robert 69, 70, 71
Dodman, Virtue 70
Dog Sign 99
Dog, The 36-42
Doidge, David and Laura 33
Domesday Book 1, 3
Doughty 58
Doughty, Harriet 33

Dove 62
Dowing or Dewing 48
Drabblegate 5
Drake, Ernest 55
Ducker, Geoffrey 74
Ducker, Samuel 58, 73, 74
Ducker, Stanley Samuel 74
Ducker's Funeral Services 74
Dunkirk 92, 93
Duson, Veronica 43
Dyball 80
Dyball, Alfred 36
Dyball, Donald 79
Dye, Elizabeth 36
Dye, Matthew 45, 50
Dye, Robert 36
Dyes House 5

Eager, John 76
Eastoe, Ernest Alfred 79
Easton, Robert 85
Ebden, James 36
Edwards, Edward 13, 14
Eggleton, Tony 36
Elesham 1
Elizabeth I 11, 43, 101
Empson, Thomas 93, 96
Ex-Servicemen's Club 64

Fairhead, Wm. Sheridan Selby 50, 52
Farmers Union 24
Farrand, Peter and Paula 23
Feathers Sign 99
Feathers, The 33-35
Feek, Dick 48, 50, 51
Felbrigg Hall 19
Felstead, Robert 92
Fenn, Annie Frances 81
Fenn, William 81
Fire Brigade Station 20
Firemen's Dinner 62
Fish, James 69
Fitt, James 85
Flanders, William 58
Flint, William 71
Flood, William Herbert 50
Follet, W.W.S. 62
Ford, 62
Foresters Hall 51
Forster, Charles 76

113

Forster, Mary 76
Forster, Thomas 76
Fox, The 96, 97
Francis, Robert 36
Frary, John 26
Freeman, Jemima 79
Freeman, John 79, 81
Fylt, William 13

Garner, Henry 13
Garrett, D.J. 13
Garrett, Daisy 13
Garrett, Edward 13
Gas Light & Coke Co. 7
Gas House Hill 2
Gathercole, Alice Emma 13
Gaunt, John of 1
Gedge, Frederick 76
Gidney, H.J. 47, 67
Gilderstone, John 23
Globe Sign 101
Globe, The 96
Gogle, James 41
Goodwin, John 58
Goodwin, Robert 71
Goodwin, Rosanna 58
Gothic House 6
Gould, Trevor 33
Goulden 62
Grange, The 5
Gray & Cooper 74
Great Flood 1912 89
Great Kirkmere 93
Green, Widow 48
Green, William 48
Greengrass, George 31
Greenwood, Richard 103
Greenwood, Ursula 29
Griffin Sign 101
Griffin, The 96
Grimson, George 58
Gurney & Co. 47

Hagon, Pauline 79
Hagon, Robert 76
Half Moon Cottage 29
Half Moon Inn 29
Half Moon Sign 99
Hall, Emma 64
Hall, Miles 60

Hall, Robert 45
Hall, Thomas 48
Hallifore, Thomas 76
Hammond, William Herbert 79
Hardy, William 50, 108
Hargrave, James 93
Harriman, John 85
Harriman, Richard 13, 16
Harrison, William 55
Harrod, James 47
Hart, Henry Gardener 29
Hart, Mary Ann 29
Hart, Phillip 69
Hart-Bowgen, J.I. 36
Harvey, Robert 94
Harvey, Thomas 93, 94
Hawes, Robert 23, 48, 104
Hawkins, Thomas 69
Heaton, Phillip 23
Herring, Robert 97
Hewitt, Emma and Charles 33
Hill, William 23
Hillingdon, Lord 17
Hogg, W.F. 36
Holman House 4
Holman Road 20
Hooks, Mary 48
Hopkins, Benjamin 56
Hopkins, John 48
Hopkins, Joseph 56
Howard, Annie 66
Howard, Len 66
Howe, Thomas 29
Howes, Martha 26
Howes, Matthew 92
Humphreys 62
Hungate Street 4, 23, 29, 31
Hutchinson, Samuel 48

Inland Revenue 17
Inn Gray's 10
Inn Lincolns 10
Inn Middle and Lower Temple 10
Inns of Court 10
Intrepreneur Pub Company 13, 23
Ives, Clement 76

Jackson, Christopher George Wilmot 29
Jannys, Robert 6
Jarvies, Robert 69

Jarvis, Edward 73
Jay, Hannah 52
Jay, William 50, 52
Jegon, Arthur 45
Jennings, John 85
Joiner, William 48
Jones, Jerry 36
Jordan, Henry 58

Kemp, Andrew and Jill 67
Kemp, Mrs 50
Kemp, William 50
Kerry, Arthur 79
Kilby, William 76
King Charles II 20
King David of Kent 9
King Edward VII 17, 34
King George VI 65
King's Head 50
King's Head sign 99
King James I 11
King, Keziah 64
King, Mary 73
Kirk, Ernest 55
Kittlebridge 45
Knoll, The 4

Lack, Thomas 48
Lancaster, Duke of 1
Lancaster Manor 13, 36
Lancum, Henry 79
Laws, Bill 36
Laxen, Richard 26, 52, 79, 82
Laxen, Annie Frances 79
Laxen, Edwin and Nadia 23
Laxen, Henry Fenn 83
Leaman, Robert 36
Legood, Hannah 60
Legood, William 60
Leoman, Thomas and Emma 102
Levick, James 48
Linen and canvas 6
Ling, James 79
Ling, Mrs James 79
Lloyd, Leah 13
Lomax, William 92
Lombe, Thomas and Philippa 13
Lovell, Thomas 92
Lovick, Elizabeth 48
Lovick, John and Mary 48

Loyal Aylsham Volunteers 41
Lubbock, Thomas 36
Lungley, Anne 85, 86
Lungley, Isaac 86

Maid's Head 96
Maid's Head Sign 101
Maiden's Bower 93, 94
Maires, Anne 31
Maltings 85
Manthorpe, Robert 29
March, A.J. 62
Market Place 1, 4, 5
Marsh, James 85
Marsham, Robert 3
Mash, Elizabeth Hayne 89
Mash, William 85, 87, 89
Mash's Row 89
Master Marriner 65
Mawston, Ronald and Shelley 33
Meddler, Robert 48
Melonie, Emily Louisa 36
Melonie, William 36
Mercantile Service 65
Middleton, Jacob 47
Milbourne, Richard 37
Mileham, William 51
Mill Lane 31
Mill Road 31
Mill Row 5
Millgate 3, 4, 7, 74, 76, 85, 102, 103
Millgate Street 85, 87
Mills 3, 85, 91
Monument, W. 62, 67
Morgan Brewery Co. Ltd. 29, 58, 66, 105
Morgan, J.B. 58
Morton, Dr. R.K. 5, 62
Mosey, Francis 13, 36
Moy, John 34
Mullinger, Samuel 36
Murton, Albert 60, 65

National Trust 4
National Union of Railymen 32
Navigation Canal 89, 94
Navigation Company 3, 41, 85
Neale, Arthur 62
Neale, E.J. 13
Neave, Walter Robert 79

115

Nelson Horace 16
Nelson, Horatio 16
New Inn Sign 99
New Inn, The 50-52
New Road 4
Newstead, Phillis 23
Newstead, William 23
Nicholls, John 76, 77
Nicholls, Robert 73
Nicholls, Stanley 76, 77
Nicholls, Susannah 76, 77
Norfolk House 4
Norfolk Regiment 62, 67
Norgate, Rachel 13
Normans 9
Norwich 1
Norwich Brewery 23, 66, 67, 79, 105
Norwich City Works 7
Norwich Road 37, 45, 47
Norwich to Cromer Turnpike 17, 41

Oakapple Day 51
Oakfield Road 51
Old Bank House 46, 47
Old Bull Motor & Cycle Works 49
Old Vicarage 5
Oliver, George 79
Ollands 96
Olliett 14
Ollyett, Simon 13
Orwell, William and Christina 102
Osborne, Robert 60

Page, Leonard G. 31
Page, Mrs G. 31
Parmeter, Francis 48, 85, 86, 107
Parmeter, Robert 3, 29, 85, 86, 103
Parmeter, Samuel 89
Parr, Curtis 58
Partridge 62
Partridge, Arthur Edward 77
Pashley, Ernest 13
Pashley, William 13
Pask & Sons 58
Pask 62
Paston 10
Patten, Edward 26
Pearson, Everett 69
Pegg, Captain 62
Pegg, Susan 39

Penfold Street 19, 20
Perry, Kevin 13
Pert 80
Peterson, John 5
Phillips, Edward 76
Phoenix 33
Pike, Peter 23
Pilgrim, Ezra 103
Pinchin, Edward 31, 96
Poll, Henry 73, 103
Poll, Samuel 48
Poll, William 48
Pond Meadow 85
Porrett, George R. 36
Porrett, John 96, 97
Postle, Ernest 29
Postle, John 29
Postle, John and Patricia 67
Pratt, William 69
Primrose, William 58, 60, 61, 105
Prince of Wales 34
Princess Victoria 17
Protestant Dissenters 26, 70
Pub Company 1406, 13
Pubmaster 79
Pumphrey 62
Pumphrey, Albert Charles 92
Pumphrey, Anna Elizabeth 92
Puncher, John 48
Puncher, William 23
Puncher, William and Mary 26
Purdy, Capt. Thms Woods 62, 64, 67
Purdy, William 48
Pye, Allen 31, 50

Queen Elizabeth I 11, 43, 101
Queen Victoria 16, 34

Rackham 62
Railway, Bure Valley 3
Railway, North Aylsham 91
Railway, South Aylsham 3, 41
Railways 3
Rannells, Widow 76
Rannells, William 60, 76, 77, 103
Raynforth, William 36
Read, Thomas 85
Red Lion Sign 100
Red Lion St. 26, 50, 52, 58, 70, 77
Red Lion, The 60-65, 77

Rental 45
Repton, Humphrey 2
Reve, Edward or Edmund 102
Riches, Richard 58
Rifle Club 24
Ringer's Dinner 56
Rippingall 62
Rippingall, Henry 13
Rising, William 23
Rix, Henry 36
Rix, Peter 37
Robert, Sir John 45
Roberts, Edmund 23
Roberts, J.M. 56
Robertson or Roberson, Richard 50
Roman Roads 9
Romans 1
Roofe, Robert 55
Rooke, John 52
Rossell, Mr 45
Rouse, Michael 33
Roy, Miss 6
Royal British Legion 6
Royal Mail 18
Royal Oak Sign 100, 101
Royal Oak, The 92-94
Rumbell, Edward 23, 96
Russell, Robert 45
Rust, Robert 48

St Michael's Church 45, 77, 83, 96, 97
St Michael's Hospital 4
Sapwell, Dr John 5
Saskatchewan 26
Savory, Henry and Hannah 29
Saxons 1
Schools 6
Scott, W.H. 47
Scotter, Samuel 50
Scottow, Jonathan 50, 96
Scrutton, Mrs S.G. 36
Scrutton, S.G. 36
Seabourne, John and Rose 13
Secker, John 13, 48
Seely 62
Sexton, Joseph I, Joseph II 29
Shaw, Dennis 31
Shepheard, Philip Candler 5
Ship Sign 100

Ship, The 73
Sir William's Lane 5
Skelton, Ian 23
Slipper, Thomas Edward 60
Smart, William 103
Smith, Dr Frederick 89
Smith, Joe 60
Smith, John 85
Smith, Richard 36
Soame, Deborah 73
Soame, Thomas 70
Sole, Frederick William 60
Some, Christopher 36
Some, George 37
Some, John 37
Some, John and Frances 36
South African War 83
Spanton, James 13, 16
Spink, Clifford 85
Spink, Thomas 39
Spinks, Mary 76
Spring Inns 23
Spurrell, Thomas 85
Spurrell, William 64
Stackwood, Robert 56
Stangroom, William Cook 76
Stapleton, Christmas 13, 18, 60
Star Inn 58, 59
Star Inn Sign 100
Steward & Patteson 23, 31, 55, 76, 77, 79, 86, 106
Stoneham, Thomas 87
Stonemasons, The 79-84
Strain, Elizabeth 50
Strain, William 50
Suckling, Rev. Benjamin 16
Swan Close 32
Swan Sign 99
Swan, The 31, 32

Tattam, Charles 13
Taverns 10
Taylor, John 55, 56
Temperance Societies 11
Tennant, Richard 96
Thompson, C.A. 36
Thrower, Captain 36
Tinkler, John U. 79
Tompson, Walter 55
Town Band 64

Town Council 1
Town Football Club 62
Town Hall 1, 41, 86
Townsend, Lord 15
Traher, Albert V. 66
Tramplet Close 45
Trunch Brewery 60, 61, 105
Tucker, Charles Cook 13
Tuddenham 55
Tuddenham, Henry John 58
Tuddenham, William 58
Tudman, Letitia 52
Turner, Sophia 66
Turnpike Road 41, 38
Tuttington 66
Twaite, Derek 36

Ulph, John 55
Ulph, Jonathan 69, 103
Ulph, Joseph 69
Ulph, Mary 69
Ulph, Sarah 55
Underwood, Charles 33
Underwood, Stephen 33
Unicorn Sign 98
Unicorn, The 23-28

VE Day 20
Vince, Harry 55
Vintners Company 11
Volunteer Corps 41
Vowte, Mary and Robert 48

Wace, John 46
Wade, Edward Rice 23
Wagsteres 45
Walker, D.L. 47
Waller, Barry and Pat 33
Want, Donald Wilfred Gordon 23
Ward, Thomas 13
Warne, Emma and Ronald 33, 34
Warne, George 33
Waterie Lane 93
Watney Mann(East Anglia) Ltd. 13, 66, 105
Watneys Brewery 23
Watson, Hiram 64
Watson, John 31, 48, 50
Wattes, Edmund 102
Weavers Way 4

Webster, Hannah 85
Webster, James 66
Webster, John 85
Wells, George 23
Wells, Theopholis 23
West End Cinema 25
West Lodge 4, 46
Wetherell, Robert 36
Wetherell, Widow 36
Wetherell, William 36
Wherries 3, 85, 92
Whiley, Walter 23
White Hart Sign 100
White Hart St. 2, 5, 66, 69, 70, 73
White Hart, The 69-71
White Horse Sign 100
White Horse, The 76, 77
Whitehouse, Paula and Graham 13
Whittacre, William & Elizabeth 13, 14
Wiggott, Benjamin 29
Williamson, Herbert James 55, 66
Williment 62
Wills, Alexander William 36
Wills, Mrs 36
Windham, William Frederick 18, 19
Wiseman, William 76
Wood, Robert 5
Woodeforde, Parson 14
Woodhouse, Edward 60, 62
Wooll-Crosse 93
Woolley, Michael and Helen 33
Workhouse 4
Workhouse Book 39
World War I 20, 89, 92
World War II 20, 89
Wrench, Rev. Jonathan 5
Wright, James 29, 92
Wright, Thomas 85
Wright, Widow 96
Wright, William 6
Wymark, Elizabeth 25
Wymark, Henry 29, 85
Wymark, James 23, 25, 29, 71

Youngs & Crawshay 92
Youngs, Crawshay & Co. 92
Youngs, Crawshay & Youngs 73, 74, 92, 107
Youngs, John & William Burt 36, 92